IMPACT OF EXTRA MARITAL RELATIONS

By

Shweta Pal

&

Neelma Kanwar

DISCOVERY PUBLISHING HOUSE PVT. LTD.

NEW DELHI-110 002

Published by:
Tilak Wasan

DISCOVERY PUBLISHING HOUSE PVT. LTD.
4831/24, Prahlad Street, Ansari Road
Darya Ganj, New Delhi-110002 (India)
Phone: +91-11-23279245, 43764432
Fax: +91-11-23253475
E-mail: parul.wasan@gmail.com
info@discoverypublishinggroup.com
web: www.discoverypublishinggroup.com

***First Edition:* 2011**
ISBN: 978-81-8356-774-9

Impact of Extra Marital Relations

Printed at:
Shree Balaji Art Press
Delhi

Preface

Extra-marital relation a pattern of behaviour that seeks satisfactions at the expense of commitment to another. It strikes at the core defining characteristics of marriage. Two people determine to share themselves with each other in a way that is unique to them and not shared by others. They agree that the levels of trust and accountability, expected of each other will be greater than found in any other of their relationship. They share physical, emotional, mental and spiritual intimacy, not found in other relationship. Their relationship is permanent and unconditional.

Extra-marital relations are relations to be made and nourished outside the marriage. Extra-marital relations are related to or being sexual intercourse between a married person and someone than his/her spouse.

Long before written history primitive class and tribes were living within small highly inter-dependent social structures. Many of there groups has some type of ceremony marking the forming of a union or marriage between two opposite sex partners. As societies evolved, the marriage bond took on increased significance within each culture. One of the most universal aspect of the marriage union to be perpeuted cross culturally was monogamy yet despite this proclivity towards marriage and insistence that the marriage partners remain monogamous, human beings have been engaging in non-monogamous activities throughout history.

When ever a person engages in a relationship with another that violates these characteristics of marriage. This

happens when the new relationship results in a breakdown of trust, develops intimacy with others that belongs in the marriage, when experiences are shared with the new person that become more important than the shared experiences in the marriage.

When one partner goes outside of the relationship for emotional, physical or other need, than the spouse may end the relationship, or forgive and stay in but either way extra-martial affair have major negative effects that can be felt for sometime.

Dr. Shweta Pal
Dr. Neelma Kunwar

Acknowledgements

My debts are great and too many especially like the debt of God, which, I cannot dare to acknowledge and who bestowed on me the courage to carry out this work.

Words can never express the indebtness but I dare to take this opportunity to pay my deep sense of gratitude, heartiest thanks and respect to **Dr. Neelma Kunwar** (D.Sc.), Associate Professor, Department of Extension Education & Communication Management (ECM), C.S. Azad University of Agriculture and Technology, Kanpur and chairperson of the advisory committee for her enthusiastic interest, outstanding co-operation, unending zeal, constant encouragement, calm endurance, diligence and constructive criticism during the entire course of investigation and preparation of this work.

I also express by heartfelt thanks and gratitude to **Dr. (Mrs.) Rekha Dayal,** Associate Professor, Department of Family Resource Management, College of Home Science, **Dr. R.N. Prasad,** Associate Professor (Statistics), Department of Agricultural Economics and Statistics and **Dr. Mukesh Srivastava**, Associate Professor, Department of Plant Pathology, C.S. Azad University of Agriculture and Technology, Kanpur, who are the members of my Advisory Committee, for their effluent efforts, timely guidance and creative suggestions during the tenure of the present study.

I express my sincere thanks and deep sense of gratitude and regards to **Mr. Arun Kumar Srivastava,** Assistant Statistician, Department of Crop Physiology and equally obliged and express my veneration to **Ms. Priya Vashishtha**

and **Ms. Renuka Singh,** Teachers, Department of ECM, C.S. Azad University of Agriculture and Technology, Kanpur, who cooperated me during my study period.

This rare moment of pride and pleasure in my life became possible due to the support of my family. From the core of heart, uncountable words of cordial veneration and gratitude and dedicated to my father **Mr. S.C. Pal** and my mother **Mrs. Kanti Pal** for their love, affection, good wishes, blessing constant encouragement and inspiration showered upon me for the achievements of my present educational assets. I also express my warmest appreciation to my younger brother "Anshu", who extended moral support, timely help and constant inspiration to me during the entire period of my study.

I offer my warmest thanks and indebtedness to my friends; Nishu, Varsha, Arti, Roli, Akanksha di, Preeti Ashvini, Praveen and all others for their constant love, help and encouragement.

My love gane the superfluous from the hearts bottom of Gungun, Jiya and Hunny for their love.

I am also grateful for the enormous affection, constant encouragement, cordial support and best wishes extended by those whose presence you can feel always at the hour of need. Their love and moral support helped me to cope up with problems and should me the path to success.

I am also thankful to **Mr. A.K.S. Sengar,** Office Secretary, Office of the Registrar, C.S. Azad University, Kanpur for neat and clean typing of this manuscript and **Mr. Ajit** for Computer designing and graphics of the data, besides other time to time help.

Lastly, the cooperation provided by the entire staff of the College of Home Science, C.S. Azad University of Agriculture and Technology and all the respondents of the study area are greatly acknowledged.

Shweta Pal

Contents

Introduction

Long before written history, primitive clans and tribes were living within small, highly inter-dependent social structures. Many of these groups had some type of ceremony marking the forming of a union or marriage between two opposite sex partners. It appears that since we began living in structured social groups, human have adhered to the belief that formal unions of two people work best for maintaining a healthy, functioning society. Within different societies, independent unions of two people were considered the best way to secure food and shelter, defend against outside aggressors, and raise offspring. As societies evolved, the marriage bond took on increased significance within each culture. One of the most universal aspects of the marriage union to be perpetuated cross-culturally was monogamy. Yet despite this proclivity towards marriage, and insistence that the marriage partners remain monogamous, human beings have been engaging in non-monogamous activities throughout history.

The loss of the high level of passion and desire that existed in the beginning of the relationship may result in boredom or develop into a feeling of apathy towards the partner. Combined with all of the other stresses and complexities of long term relationships, such as financial problems, raising

children, job changes, death of family members, change in status, etc., the loss of passion may lead to a desire to rediscover it in the start of a new relationship.

So it may not be the desire to experience the "new" or "forbidden" sexual relationship, but rather the need to re-experience the intense level of passion and the feeling of being "in love" and all which that implies, that leads to affairs. Therefore, extra-marital affairs may be the result of an inability to maintain a satisfying emotional relationship with a partner over a long period of time, and not due to a need for sexual variety. Possibly our need for intense emotional experiences leads to a desire to rediscover the feelings that come at the start of a new love relationship. Whether it is our expectation that passion remain or our inability to maintain passion easily in long term relationships, the loss of it appears to be a major factor in the initiation of affairs. Once initiated, the high level of passion experienced in affairs appears to be a powerful component in the maintaining them.

Few famous examples of "extra-marital affairs", star of the millennium Amitabh Bachhan; Princess of Wales Diana; Former President of USA Bill Clinton; former English cricketer Ian Botham, cricketer Shane Warne, cricketer turned politician Imran Khan and Liquor Baron Vijaya Mallya .... they are carrying an image of a "play-boy". May celebrities from entertainment industry; sportsmen and politicians across the globe are into such type of relations.

Definition

Extra-marital relations are relations to be made and nourished outside the marriage. Extra-marital relations are related to or being sexual intercourse between a married person and someone other than his/her spouse.

Extra-marital relation is a pattern of behaviour that seeks satisfactions at the expense of commitment to another. It strikes at the core defining characteristics of marriage. Two people determine to share themselves with each other in a

way that is unique to them and not shared by others. They agree that the levels of trust and accountability, expected of each other will be greater than found in any other of their relationships. They share physical, emotional, mental, and spiritual intimacy, not found in other relationship. Their relationship is permanent and unconditional.

Extra-marital Relations

Whenever a person engages in a relationship with another that violates these characteristics of marriage. This happens when the new relationship results in a breakdown of trust; develops intimacy with another that belongs in the marriage; when experiences are shared with the new person that become more important than the shared experiences in the marriage. Infidelity can occur without sex. Simply stated, marriage is a commitment to seek mutual fulfilment to make your own satisfaction contingent on your spouse's. The first steps taken when infidelity occurs are (1) to decide to seek fulfilment through someone else and (2) to decide to do this secretly. In a sense, whatever a person decides to give to a new partner outside the marriage is taken from his or her spouse, time, money, special experiences, confidences, or intimacies.

If the interpersonal relationship was satisfying for both partners, and passion was still an integral part of the relationship, the need to experience diversified or new sexual partner may not exist. It is clearly indicated that people's diminished feeling for their partner led them to become involved in the extra-marital relation. Specifically, many people report feeling unappreciated, ignored, sexually frustrated and no longer desirable to their partners. They almost invariably say that they are no longer "in love" with their partners and lack the level of intimacy that they once had. In almost all cases, the married member of an affair has reported that they feel "more alive", "more sexually appealing" and "more appreciated" by their lovers than by their spouses.

Gender Differences in how Men and Women View Extra-marital Relations

There are some gender differences in how men and women view extra-marital relationships, although these are generalizations, not true in every instance. Women seem to be drawn into adulterous relationships initially through emotional attachments, while men are more likely attracted sexually. Interestingly, each gender tends to assume that the other is acting out of the same motivation as they are likely to themselves. Women assume that their husband has become emotionally attached to another woman, when his interest may be primarily physical. Men make the mistake of thinking that their wife's relationship with another man is safe if she shows no physical attraction to him (*Psychology Today*, Aug. 1998). These issues may need to be addressed in the recovery process in order that both husband and wife can understand the development of the extra-marital relationship.

There is a famous Hindi saying in northern India which translate, literally means:

"The other person's wife and his own children always appear prettier to a man."

The first half of this saying hints only at one form of extra-marital sexual affairs such relations, in fact develop more frequently between married men and unmarried women, and between married women and bachelors. Married men having affairs with married women are less common, though its frequency varies depending on the couple's social class and milieu.

In tribal and in lower castes; in lower economic strata of society women practices sex in legalized way. Due to poverty it is accepted in their society. They practice sex for economic reasons, either they are married or not. Their family allows them to do so. In higher class, open society is there, they enjoy their life as they want. Man/women both attend clubs, night parties, share each other's wife, husbands and it is popularly known as wife swapping. It is a status symbol of high society so sex outside the marriage bond is common in

lower castes and high society. In lower castes it is due to economic crisis and in higher society it is a status symbol. So extra-marital relations are very common and socially accepted in society now-a-days.

Why do People have Affairs?

There is a multitude of reasons that operate in the development of extra-marital relations. The trigger may be an attraction generally physical in nature but camouflaged by other overt manifestations. The fundamental reason, of course, is sex. The driving force is either unsaturated sexual desire or craving for a variety in sex life. To say that one can have 'platonic' extra-marital relations is a façade. It doesn't happen in everyday life.

The indication is that the desire for a new sexual experience is not the initial motive for looking outside the marriage, but rather comes after the breakdown of the emotional relationship. Only then, after there has been an eroding of the interpersonal relationship, including a loss of passion, lack of intimacy, and loss of emotional and sexual satisfaction, does the dissatisfied partner look for a new lover to fulfill their needs.

The situations, which most commonly lead to extra-marital relations are :

Disharmony in Married Life

This can stem from a variety of reasons. However, the commonest cause for a disturbed family environment is an unsatisfactory sex life. Other causes are incompatibility between partners; financial problems and all-too-common social problems like the "in-law" syndrome. In such situations, the person seeks some solace outside the marriage.

A lousy sex life means that unfulfilled sexual desires keep accumulating and ultimately, the frustrated man or woman looks for a outlet. This outlet is often found in a colleague or a close relative. What starts out as a physiological cause

slowly leads to a physical solution, which could turn complicated.

Proximity at the Workplace

Probably the commonest factor – especially in urban settings. In recent years, a flood of women have joined the workforce, either to start their own business, fulfill their own ambitions or seek economic independence. This trend is obviously increasing as the pressures of enhancing the family income grow. Increasing female literacy is providing more work opportunities. What this has done is facilitate contact between male and female colleagues, in many cases in a one-on-one situation or at least in close proximity to each other. Mutual attraction is a logical and natural occurrence. To begin with, the physical virtues of a colleague are responsible for this though it is often camouflaged with the façade of intellectual compatibility. Infatuations like this ultimately lead to the bedroom.

Obviously, colleagues with troubled married lives are more susceptible. However, in quite a few cases, it starts off with oversexed males looking for a fling. Beware the male who says he is just looking for a shoulder to cry on because of differences with his wife. The search for solace and sympathy is, coincidentally, always directed at single women. It's an age-old ploy and it is surprising how many well-educated, highly intelligent women fall into this trap.

High Expectations from Marriage

In quite a few cases, the proclivity towards having an affair is a symptom of an individual's inability to find satisfaction in a long-term relationship because of the high expectations placed on the relationship or the spouse initially. Some people find it difficult if not impossible to remain 'in love' with their partners as they grow older and mature. This 'falling out of love' can lead to the search for a new sexual partner or a different sexual experience.

Change in Circumstance

Generally happens to people on the fast lane that suddenly achieves professional and financial success or receives a financial windfall which brings overnight riches. The sudden change in circumstance provides an incentive for some people to look for another intimate relationship or multiple sex partners. A man or woman who is successful, a celebrity and much admired becomes a target for the opposite sex.

Loss of Passion

The loss of the high level of passion and desire that first attracted two people to each other can, over a period of time, drift into boredom and develop into a feeling of apathy towards the partner. Combined with all the other stresses and complexities of long-term relationships—financial problems, raising demanding children, job changes, changes in status, loss of position—it may lead to a desire to rediscover lost passion in the arms of someone new.

Extended Periods Away from Home

Always due to reasons of work. This factor operates in cases where the husband/wife has to be frequently away on business tours or to attend conferences or is forced to stay away from the spouse due to the place of work being distant. Loyalty to the partner acts as a controlling force in such situations. However, sexual desire is one of the strongest physiological drives. We are, after all, descendants of Adam and Eve. The urge to stray among men and women who spend time traveling abroad or in different cities is often irresistible. More so since the belief is that he/she won't get caught if they have a sexual encounter in a foreign or distant city.

Loneliness and Depression

This can occur for a variety of reasons. These are the periods, which make a person emotionally weak and vulnerable. A

helping hand or a shoulder to cry on if available in such times can create a situation of intimacy and lead to the initiation of an extra-marital relationship. Quite frequently, the initiator is a man and often the "victim"—already under the obligation of the "helper" just can't resist the slowly increasing advances. Ultimately, culmination may be in the form of yet another extra-marital relation.

Fulfilling a Sexual Fantasy

Usually boils down to an urge to introduce variety in one's sex life. Often the cause is experimentation with sexual fantasies which is not possible with the partner. In a majority of cases, whether it is the man or a woman attempting to fulfil a sexual fantasy, it is generally restricted to a one-night stand. Obviously in these situations, both the partners are quite willing and if they enjoy the experience, then the possibility of a longer-term relationship exists. Very often this happens between a middle aged, married male and a young, unmarried woman. Physical factors are the primary force in such scenarios.

Favours Sought or Granted

Though not initially seen as an "affair", this scenario does take place more frequently in countries where politicians or people in power can grant favours to overly-ambitious women or, in many cases, wives acting on behalf of their husbands. Though this is more like a sex worker selling herself, there are times when the favours multiply and the temptation is too great. That's when such relationships can convert into protracted extra-marital relations. Usually between an influential married man or woman with a married woman or man.

Revival of an Old Flame

One fine day, you bump into an old flame and something strange happens. The old chemistry starts working again. The trigger is usually a psychological dependency

experienced in the old days. The former acquaintance might just supply the psychological cushion that may be deficient in one's married life. If these meetings continue unabated, extra-marital relations can easily develop. Apparently, someone who is not happy in his/her married life is more likely to succumb to this. The fundamental force is the sexual drive, specially if the earlier relationship included sex that was fulfilling and enjoyable.

Physical Attraction

A substantial number of people end up having extra-marital relations due to sheer physical attraction. These usually develop among people of the same social circle or between persons belonging to the same extended household.

How Prevalent are Affairs ?

Conservative estimates are that 60 per cent of men and 40 per cent of women will have an extra-marital affair. These figures are even more significant when we consider the total number of marriages involved—since it's unlikely that all the men and women having affairs happen to be married to each other. "if even half of the women having affairs (or 20%) are married to men not included in the 60 per cent having affairs then at least one partner will have an affair in approximately 80 per cent of all marriages. But we need to take a closer look at the statistics on affairs to determine what they can contribute to an understanding of our sexual patterns. While affairs happen in non-marital, "committed" relationships as well as within marriage, most of the statistics deal only with "extra-marital" affairs. These statistics began with Kinsey's reports in the 1940s and early 1950s. Kinsey's samples included 5,000 men and showed that by age 40, 50 per cent of the men had experienced extra-marital sexual intercourse. Kinsey's original samples of 6000 women showed that by age 40, 26 per cent of the women had experienced extra-marital sexual intercourse.

Affairs are glamorized in movies, soap operas, romance novels, and TV shows of all kinds. Public disclosure of public figures having affairs is headline news because we are fascinated and titillated by hearing of other's affairs.

People are bombarded with images of women as sex objects in advertising and marketing campaigns. Over and over, the message to men is that the good life includes a parade of sexy women in their lives. Women inadvertently buy into this image and strive to achieve it.

Types of Extra-marital Affairs

There are many types of extra-marital affairs and while all of them are terrible betrayals of the trust and love between the couple, it directly affects the chances for survival of the marriage. Affairs are loaded with romanticism, morality, mythology and intense emotions.

The first kind of affair is what is called as 'One Night Stand'. This mostly happens unintentionally and may not necessarily be a sexual affair at all. It happens when one person feels ignores in the relationship and just for sometime needs to be away from the tension and pressure.

The second kind of affair is known as 'Emotional Outbreak Affair'. This generally happens when the marriage is experiencing problems and during those times one partner turns towards a friend or companion of the opposite sex for emotional help and comfort.

The third kind of affair is known as "Emotional Sexual Affair" and this affair causes lot of heart break and problems because in such type of affair the unfaithful spouse not only gives the body but also the heart and there are slim chances of reunion.

The fourth kind of affair is "Sexual addiction Affair" sexual addicts use sex over and over again to number of pair and emptiness, much like alcoholics use alcohol. Among married people, men are sexual addicts more often than women. The other affair happen because of boredom, lack of communication, sexual experimentation, to combat a sense of loss that can come to with ageing, depression etc.

Advantages of Extra-marital Relations

Sometimes extra-marital relations are beneficial for people. The fact is that there have been as many advantages given for affairs as there are people engaging in them are as follows :

(1) **Reduce loneliness :** Many people live away from home for long period of time due to their job. So they engage in extra-marital relationship for fulfil their loneliness of life.

(2) **Fulfil emotional emptiness :** In most of the marriages it is inability to maintain a satisfying emotional relationship with a spouse over a long period of time so possibly their need for intense emotional experiences leads to a desire to rediscover the feelings that come at the start of a new love relationship outside the marriage.

(3) **New sexual opportunity :** In most of the marriages many people feeling unappreciated ignored sexually frustrated and no longer desirable to their partners. So people go outside the marriage for fulfil our need and variety for sex.

(4) **More alive, more sexually appealing and more appreciated :** The loss of the high level of passion and desire may result in boredom or develop into a feeling of apathy towards partner. Combined with all of the other stresses and complexities of long-term marital relationships such as financial problems, raising children, job changes etc. may lead to desire to rediscover it in the new relationship outside the marriage.

In almost cases the married member having an affair, they feel "more alive", "more sexually appealing" and "more appreciated" by their lovers than by their spouses.

(5) **Economic support :** In many cases of extra-marital relation one partner have a highly economic status it gives support to other partner economically.

Disadvantages of Extra-marital Relations

When one partner goes outside of the relationship for emotional, physical or other need, than the spouse may end the relationship, or forgive and stay in but either way extra-marital affair have major negative effects that can be felt for sometime.

(*i*) Damage of self-esteem
(*ii*) Lack of trust
(*iii*) Sense of instability
(*iv*) Roller coaster of emotions
(*v*) The ripple effect and
(*vi*) Emotional disturbance

Stress of Extra-marital Relationship

The telling effect of your deteriorating marital relationship will manifest as insomnia, hypertension and depression. The possible cause may be endless, but an unaffectionate and unforgiving attitude of your spouse or extra-marital relationship or your inability to find a quality time with your spouse may cause stress.

Since the relationship differs from person to person or in other words the relationship depends on the nature of the person, it is important to handle your stress in your marital relationship at the initial stage itself. You can let your spouse know the exact issue and an honest communication can solve the problem at its initial stage itself. You should also try to change your rigid attitude and practice a flexible approach, which will definitely pave way for your spouse also to reciprocate marriage for someone who can meet them.

Effect on Family and Children

When a parent have extra-marital relations then it also affects his/her children because he/she will not pay full attention towards them and may be he/she will not perform his/her duties towards his/her children.

When husband has extra-marital relation then it affects emotionally his wife because she becomes emotionally disturb. Emotional support is very essential and when wife does not find this and physical attachment from her husband she feels insecure.

Despite international and national conventions prohibiting discrimination against any child and imposing responsibilities on parents, society and state to protect it in every manner, an illegitimate child born out of an extra-marital relation is still exposed to enormous social, emotional and legal deprivation. While the parents can foresee the consequences of their socially and legally disapproved alliance in the form of extra-marital relation, the child has no choice in the matter. The sharing of the physical company and properties between children born outside wedlock would be at the expense of the family, and thus the peace and stability of the marriage would be threatened. Justice Douglas in 1968 stated that :

> "illegitimate children are not non-persons. They are humans and have their being".

The child, eventually, after witnessing the hostile environment at home and the parental animosity resulting from the extra-marital of either of the parents, breaks down under the strain of conflict. The child's distress may take the form of school related problems, anxiety, depression, bullying, victimization and sometimes even health related illness. Eventually, the parents must be brought along to understand that their antagonistic tug of war is the toxicity hurting their child. Finally the child needs to be brought into a session with both the parents whether they demonstrate their maturity by cooperating for the child's mental development and growth by giving him/her the necessary family environment and equal love, care and support from both the parents thus to extinguish any insecurities or mental pressure the child might be undergoing. Apart from the legal recognition of the difference in status of a child born within and outside wedlock, it is the societal rejection and practical problems which add to the hardship of such children. These

can be witnessed in several matters such as birth registration, name, school admission, marriage and so on. Under article 7(1) of the Convention on Child Rights (1989) states that,

> "the child shall be registered immediately after birth and shall have the right to a name, the right to acquire a nationality and as far as possible, the right to know and be cared by his or her parents."

Constraints of Extra-marital Relations to Maintaining Future

The lack of social acceptance for open marriage deals with the generally negative attitudes toward open marriage in Western societies, the reasons for those negative attitudes, and the consequences of those negative attitudes for couples in open marriages.

Surveys show large majorities of people disapprove of extra-marital sexual activity. A few studies show people specifically disapprove of open marriages. Critics have put forward moral, medical, and psychological objections to open marriages. The lack of social acceptance places pressure on couples to hide their open marriages from family, friends, and colleagues. This may limit their social support network, resulting in a loss of psychological and physical health benefits:

(*i*) Evidence of disapproval

(*ii*) Religious objections

(*iii*) Health concerns

(*iv*) Psychological concerns.

(*v*) Loss of social support

(*i*) Evidence of disapproval : Disapproval of extra-marital sex does not specifically imply disapproval of open marriage, since open marriage does not always involve extra-marital sex. Very large majorities of people disapprove of extra-marital sex in general and substantial majorities feel open marriage is wrong even when the spouses agree to it.

(*ii*) **Religious objections :** Some critics object to open marriages on the ground that open marriages violate religious principles e.g. open marriage clearly contradict traditional Christian doctrine.

(*iii*) **Health concern :** Engaging in sex with a greater number of partners increases the risk of sexually transmitted diseases, including HIV/AIDS. Since open marriage increase the number of sex partners by allowing extra-marital relationships, open marriage increase the risk of sexually transmitted diseases. This has led some people to reject open marriage as a legitimate life style.

(*iv*) **Psychological concern :** Several authors consider open marriages to be physiologically damaging. They claim sexual non-monogamy proves too difficult for most couples to manager and their relationship suffer as consequences.

(*v*) **Loss of social support :** Due to strong social disapproval of open marriages, people in open marriages frequently try to hide their lifestyle to family, friends and colleagues. Keeping their lifestyles secret reduces the amount of social support available to people in open marriages strong social disapproval of open marriage may lead to a loss of psychological and health benefits for couples in open marriages.

Five Steps to Surviving an Extra-marital Affairs

1. Recognize your role. If your spouse had an emotional affair or was physically unfaithful, try to understand how and why your marriage was suffering. Two people contribute to an unhappy marriage. Consider marital counseling to help you and your spouse see how, why and when your relationship faltered.
2. Be open to change. Neither you nor your spouse is perfect, but you both need to be open to recognizing your flaws and making changes that will improve your communication, interaction, and commitment.

3. Limit your questions. According to Gary Neuman (author of *Emotional Infidelity. How to avoid* it), "the issues is controversial among marital therapists." You may feel that you can deal with the extra-marital affair better if you know the details, yet knowing everything can prolong the pain. Dr. Neuman recommends discussing the questions that will help you survive marital infidelity:

   "There are some questions you are entitled to know the answers to, "says Gary Neuman. These include, who was it, how did you meet, how long did the relationship last, do you have a relationship now, does anyone else know, and why did you have the affair."

4. Don't keep bringing the extra-marital affair up. After you've received a genuine apology and a reassurance that it'll never happen again, put it behind you. Don't bring it up during arguments or discussions.

5. Resolve to move on. Let go of the past after you've created a plan for surviving infidelity. See the extra-marital affair as a terrible mistake when your marriage was suffering – and as a vehicle for creating a more vibrant, honest, and trusting marriage.

Keeping the above explanations in mind, the present study was undertaken to know the advantages of extra-marital relationships in Indian community with following objectives:

1. Socio-economic status of male and female.
2. Opinions of gender discrimination about extra-marital relations.
3. Assess the advantage and disadvantage of extra-marital relations.
4. Psychological stress of extra-marital relationship.
5. Constraints of extra-marital relations to maintain in future.

JUSTIFICATION OF THE STUDY

Extra-marital relations are increasing. Sometimes these relations are beneficial for people because it reduces loneliness give support during mental stress, economic problems.

Now-a-days due to education, economic independence, marriage, age has been increased. Men and women work together, so intimate friendship is increasing. Today's stressful life pattern which increases health problems, intimate friendship is very useful because it is a stress buster too.

Extra-marital affairs can cause a ripple effect in life. People may find themselves looking differently at their job, their friends, and their life choices. This can be either positive or negative, but most victims of an affair say that it brought on changes in all other areas of their lives.

Review of Literature

The review of literature is the basis of most of the research. "The literature in any field forms the foundation upon which all future work is built". Review of related literature of the study has become an established practice of all research report but this should not be taken as mere practice or traditions in writing research process. Briefly it may be pointed out that review of related literature gives an insight into the problems. The important aspect of this tradition is that the researcher come to know about the present position of the problem and also the explored and unexplored aspect of the problem. It was in view of these considerations that the investigator shifted the pages of journals, abstracts, so the different aspect of problem may be elaborated.

Mortimer and Sorenson (1999) assumed that employment of wives had a variety of consequences, such as harming marital relations or children's development.

Fehr (1999) says in extra-marital relationship differences are caused by such things as betrayal of trust.

Meyer, Cathy (1999) stated that victim of an affair will find it difficult to trust. Even if this relationship ends, and another begins, the baggage of infidelity can follow.

Wittkower, E.D. (1999) has shown that extra-marital affairs can cause a ripple effect in life. People may find themselves looking differently at their job, their friends, their life choices.

Shirley and Thomas (1999) study has been focused traditional sex roles that influence the expression of sexuality and emotionality in premarital and marital relationship also appear to operate extra-marital relation.

Bienko, M. (1999) has suggested that fidelity is rarely addressed as an explicit dimension of family love although it is normally an implied obligation of marriage. It is certainly an important factor in understanding the stability or instability of marriage in a particular society. Polish civil and canon law are reviewed for their statements on fidelity.

Glass and Wright (1999) found on research the extra-marital relations is extremely complex, there are interactional effects among study variables, and, as a result, the phenomenon is not easily understood in a simplistic or linear fashion. Further, practitioners must exercise caution in using this information as they work with couples and individuals, as these research findings are not absolute truth, rather they are tentative ideas about what might be going on in the lives of clients. It is important to note that even though we review the broad subject of infidelity, studies use the term differently and apply it to diverse types of relationships.

Gloss (1999) emphasized that extra-marital affair is an emotional out break affair. This generally happens when the marriage is experiencing problems and during those times one partners turns towards a friend or companion of the opposite sex.

Regan (2000) said that one can be sexually attracted without being in love but you are not likely to be in love in the absence of sexual attraction.

Broode, J. (2000) said that extra-marital relation is a sexual addition. Sexual addicts use sex over and over again to number of person.

Anon, Paris and Anon (2000) found that engage in extra-marital relationship increase work efficiency and give emotional support.

Zinskin and Zinskin (2000) reported that co-marital sex refers to any type of extra-marital sex in which knowledge and consent is shared with the spouse.

Joyner and Udry (2000) reported that when one partner go outside the marriage than common consequences is insomnia, manifest, hypertension and depression.

Weis and Jurich (2000) used stepwise regression analysis to explore several factors that influence individual's attitudes toward extra-marital sex. Study shows that people who are well educated, who are from large metropolitan areas, who have permissive attitudes about premarital sex, and who are either single or dissatisfied with their marital relationship, are relatively more accepting of extra-marital relationships. They found that the size of community was a significant direct predictor of extra-marital attitudes even more so than marital satisfaction or status.

Kirn, Clay (2000) describes the proclivity towards having an affair is a symptom of an individual inability to find satisfaction in a long term relationship because of the high expectations placed on the relationship or the spouse initially.

Sprecher, Susan (2000) reported in research conducted by National Institute of Mental Health indicated that the participants "perceptions of the outcome of this type of extra-marital relationship dependent on the gender of the married person/single friend. Participants were more likely to believe that the married person loved the extra-marital partner, was committed to the extra-marital relationship and would marry the extra-marital partner, if the married person was a woman rather than a man. The investment manipulations had no effect on participants" perceptions of the relationship. The results were discussed as they relate to other beliefs about male vs. female sexuality.

Bhattacharjee, J. and R.S. Gupta (2000) reported that heterosexual act with person other than the legal spouse is very much prevalent among this group of middle class professionals. This situation is conductive for the spread of HIV infection among general population and may adversely influence the sexual attitudes of students. The study, therefore, suggest that besides intensifying the health education on HIV/AIDS, serious considerations about the sexual behaviours of school teachers are needed.

Ralph, A. Meyering (2001), study has found statistically significant difference between males and females were found on factors influencing extra-marital sexual relationships. It was found that man have greater expectation of personal involvement, are strongly influenced by perceived pay offs, and are more likely to respond to what they regard as justifications for their behaviour. Women are more responsive to risks which they see as more likely to occur and to be more destructive.

Durex's (2001) made to show showed large majorities of people disapprove of extra-marital sexual activity. The lack of social acceptance places pressure on couples to hide their open marriages from family, friends and colleagues. This may limit their social support network, resulting in a loss of psychological and physical health benefits.

Gwen (2001) study has been focused that extra-marital affairs happen because of boredom, lack of communication, sexual experimentation to combat a sense of loss that can come to with ageing, depression etc. in marital relationship.

Robinson (2001) emphasized upon to go from non-marital to extra-marital relationship is to make a major transition.

Atkins and Dimidijan (2001) said that infidelity is a subject that confronts couple therapists regularly in their clinical practices. It can be a confusing and heart wrenching experience for all involved, including the therapist who may have his or her own personal fears and values related to infidelity. Couple therapists who stay abreast of current

research literature may find themselves frustrated when they attempt to assimilate the research findings on infidelity. There are limitations in methodologies, conflicting results and information that is of little practical value in the therapy room.

Wiederman, Michael W. (2001) emphasized on who have ever been married were analyzed with regard to incidence, prevalence, and correlates of extra-marital sex (EMS). Men were more likely than women to report ever engaging in extra-marital sex. Except for the oldest cohort, lifetime incidence of EMS increased with age for men, whereas for woman there was an apparently curvilinear relationship such that lifetime incidence of EMS was greatest among those 30-50 years of age. Those who have ever been divorced, and those with greater attitudinal acceptance of EMS, had higher incidence of extra-marital sex, had higher incidence of extra-marital sex compared to those who have not been divorced and those reporting greater disapproval of extra-marital sex with regard to possible gender differences, men and women who denied ever engaging in extra-marital sex did not differ in their attitude about extra-marital sex. Just as men and women who reported having experienced extra-marital sex did not differ in their attitudes. The results are discussed in relation to previous research and unanswered questions left for further investigation.

Singh, Bir (2002), married men having affair with married women is less common though its frequency varies depending on the couple's social class and milieu.

S.P. and Wright (2002) studied that some person make EMR to remove our anxiety and stress. EMR helps to cope up with the other problem and person feel happy.

Singh, Bir (2002) analysed that extra-marital affair develop more frequently between married men and unmarried women, and between married women and bachelors. Married men having affairs with married women is less common, though its frequency varies depending on the couples social class and milieu.

Vaughan, Peggy (2002) stated that conservative estimates are that 60 per cent of men and 40 per cent women will have an extra-marital affair. Then at least one partner will have an affair in approximately 80 per cent of all marriages.

Kinsey et al. (2002) found that approximately one third of men and one fifth of women had extra-marital intercourse. In the three decades following the Kinsey reports numerous sex surveys were conducted with convenience samples. In general, the results of these subsequent surveys were either congruent with the Kinsey group's findings or revealed a greater incidence of extra-marital sex.

Walster, Elaine and G. William Walster (2002) said that equity theory has recently been found to be a useful framework for understanding the effects of imbalances in intimate contractual relationships such as marriage. Equitable couples seem to be happier, more satisfied with their relationship and more confident that it will last than are their more mismatched i.e. inequitable, counterparts. Furthermore, inequitable couples predictably act to set things right in their marriage. They either restore actual equity to the relationship or psychologically set their relationship in balance.

Layton, Debbie (2002) indicated that respondents diminished "feelings" for their partner led them to become involved in the extra-marital relationship specifically, many people report feeling unappreciated, ignored, sexually frustrated and no longer desirable to their partners. They almost invariably say that they are no longer "in love" with their partners and lack the level of intimacy that they once had. In almost all cases the married member of an affair has reported to me that they feel "more alive", "more sexually appealing" and "more appreciated" by their lovers than by their spouses.

Mensch, Barbara S. (2002) said to extend the research on Vietnamese youth has been conducted. It has been concerned with unprotected and unsanctioned sexual

activities and its health consequences, namely abortion and sexually transmitted diseases specially HIV or the population community.

Singh, Bir (2002) suggests that the husband and the wife are equally to blame for getting into extramarital affairs; the scenario in India is slightly different. In our experience, more often than not, it is the husband who strays. This is undoubtedly due to the dominance of the male in existing socio-economic environment.

Megan, Sweeney (2003) stated that "it is interesting to note the number of men in Teachman's sample who experienced extra-marital sex with multiple partner, rather than just with their wife's.

Strean, Herbert (2003) assumed that extra-marital affairs are however are unstable and fail to resolve conflicts.

Piercy, Fred P. Piercy (2003) concluded the people are using the internet more frequently to form friendships and romances and to initiate affairs. In the present article, the authors provide a critical review of the literature on internet infidelity. The authors examine articles that focus on the definition of internet infidelity, attitudes towards it, factors contributing to it, treatment and/or any information about the impact of internet infidelity on couples and families. The authors discuss the evolving use of the computer in sexual interactions and briefly summarize and critique the existing treatment methods. Recommendations for future directions in theory, research and practice are presented.

Buss and Schmitt (2004) reported that men are more willing than women to have sex with someone they have known for a day or less, but women prefer to know some one for a longer period before becoming intimate.

Pestrak, Victor A. and Don Martin (2004) study focused on extra-marital sex in the marital system often provides difficult dilemmas for marital therapists in regard to treatment approaches. The authors examine various

motivational and perceptual aspects among spouses for engaging in sexual activity outside the marriage. Implications for both research and treatment are discussed.

Sharma, Sanjeev (2005) indicated that extra-marital affairs based solely on desire for new sexual partners is a very small percentage of the total number of affairs specifically of the over 4300 respondents that have completed my questionnaire over 90 per cent have reported that the affair is based on emotional needs not being met within the marital relationship, and not sexually motivated reasons.

Blow, Adrian J. and Mc Gannon Hall (2005) study reveals that infidelity is perhaps the most complex issue encountered by couple therapists. Although clinical literature, opinion and speculation on this topic are abundant, research literature is sparse. What little available research exists is, in most cases, neither robust nor helpful to the practicing therapist. This article provides, in both narrative and table format a comprehensive methodological review of the available research literature on infidelity. Topics addressed in the narrative include the lack of a consensus on the definition of infidelity; design challenges, such as retrospective research, confidentiality measures, and variables, and sampling issues, such as diversity and randomization.

Swenson, Greg (2005) shows that infidelity may result of deviant character development, such that a person thrives on dishonesty and taking advantage of others. Some people derive a perverted satisfaction from having secret relationship, accumulating sexual conquests, or deceiving their spouse. Infidelity can also be a result of sexual addiction, a condition in which sexual gratification is sought compulsively in a frequency or manner not available in the marriage

Priya Devi R. (2006) explains the extra-marital affair is the most prevalent problem that is engrained in the society from time immemorial. If is only that then no one spoke about

it and today people don't hesitate to talk about it. Today it is the most common issue that frequents the doors of the marital therapist and the psychiatrists posing a challenge, as it is a traumatic interpersonal problem with intricate entanglements that seeks solutions with maximum efficacy.

Kienlen (2006) emphasized on emotional cheating. Emotional cheating can be difficult to wrap your mind around. It's not like to real affair (with intercourse) or a "sort-of-but-not really" affair (everything but the intercourse). Emotional infidelity doesn't necessarily break spoken comes, create unwanted pregnancies, or spread sexually transmitted diseases. Emotional cheating can't always be spotted in traditional ways.

Powell, Blaine (2006) says that extra-marital affairs may be symptom of our inability to find satisfaction in our long term relationships because of the expectations we place on the marriage in the first place. If the relationship doesn't lineup to ideal about love conquering all, the problem may not be with the relationship but with your ideals.

Pawlik, Laurie (2007) said that women were usually the ones who push the relationship further. Women want relationships friendship to love, from computer to reality women tend to get more emotionally involved a emotionally invested than men. Men on the other hand see the internet relationships or emotional part of their lives – a nice part, but just one part. Women envision soul mates or life partner fun.

Wiser, Bud (2007) focused on extra-marital affair is a 'one-night stand',. This mostly happens unintentionally and may not necessarily be a sexual affair at all.

Lovin, Smith, Lynn (2007) described that human marry as per social content and are supposed to stay with the mates along the life. But in reality it does not always happen as expected. Some people get involved in extra-marital affairs. In most of the case the core reason of the affair is sudden rush of physical attraction on monotony in conjugal life.

Soulen, R.N. (2008) shows that statistics may not reveal the exact truth about cheating, affair and infidelity but they at least do give us an idea. If they are to believed them the scenario, as far as marriage, cheating and infidelity is concerned is scary. On an average, 40 per cent of the females and 60 per cent of the males in America indulge in cheating extramarital affairs and commit infidelity. Clubbing those numbers together, about 80 per cent of the marriages have at one point of time or the other, cheating partners.

Smith, Robert E. (2008) focused on the most common pattern followed by the people involved in extra-marital affairs and cheating is denial. They refuse to acknowledge the fact their relationship is in the doldrums because of their affair, cheating, infidelity and needs to be worked upon. Realize that ignorance is not always bliss when it comes to extra-marital affairs, infidelity and cheating. Ignoring the fact that the marriage is going in the wrong direction is pushing it in that direction further.

Menaghan Elizabeth G. (2008) explained that the extra-marital union means any longer lasting union of a man and a woman who have not concluded marriage provided that there are no reasons suggesting that a matrimonial union of the aforementioned persons would be null. Such a union has the some consequences concerning the relations governed by the marriage and Family Relations Act (joint properly obligation of supporting the partner who is not capable of supporting himself/herself, care for children) as if the aforementioned individuals de facto married. The conditions for such a union are given in the definition longer period a man and a woman, no reasons suggesting the invalidity of a marriage.

Safranski, Misha (2009) says that an extra-marital affair affects families in a multitude of ways. One of the most devastating effects in the sense of betrayal that the spouse feels upon learning of the affair. Some spouse may experience feelings of inadequacy, along with questions about whether

they did something wrong to cause the infidelity. Once some time has passed and both partners, emotions have cooled down, the level of resentment usually fades as the couple decides to either heal the marriage or move on.

Safranski, Misha (2009) explained that extra-marital affairs cause problems not only in the husband and wife's relationship but with daily home life. Even if the betrayed spouse does not know of the affair, its effects are still stark. The effects of extra-marital affairs are like tentacles that reach into nearly aspects of the family's life.

Roid, Anna (2009) says that one of the strange thing about infidelity is that in most cases cheaters have no intention of ending their marriage and breaking up their families. In fact, cheaters don't stop loving their spouses. However, they still go for it. Why ? It's possible that monogamy might not be part of our nature as human being. People need variety in everything, including their sexual life. After spending a number of years together marital cohabitation becomes a routine, the spark is gone, replaced by a dull sense of duty.

Roid, Anna (2009) says that another reason of infidelity is job related. The average person spends about one third of their life at work. This means having constant interaction with colleagues, bosses, partners, clients etc. Everyone wants these relationships to be enjoyable and friendly, not only for their career but for other reason as well, like feeling good about yourself, avoiding stress and so on. Naturally, such close relations with someone at work can transform into something even closer. But having an affair at work does not necessarily indicate that the person stopped loving their spouse or that their extra-marital relationship will ever develop into something more serious.

Profile of the Study Area

Prior to discuss the findings of the study on "Impact of Extra-Marital Relations", it is essential to sketch briefly the salient features.

District Kanpur

Kanpur is said to be the corruption of Kanhaiyapur or Kanhpur, which was an unimportant village till its first contact with the British. According to a local tradition, the name of Kanhpur Kohna owes its origin to Hindu Singh, Raja of Sachendi, who came here about 1750, to bathe in the holy river, the Ganga and established a village, which he (possibly) named Kanhpur, the name becoming changed to Kanpur in the course of time.

Location

The district of Kanpur occupies the north-western part of the Allahabad division and belongs to the tract known as the lower doab (which comprises the eastern extremity of the strip of country lying between the Ganga and the Yamuna rivers). In shape, it is an irregular quadrilateral and lies between the parallel of 25°26′ and 26°58′ north latitude and 70°31′ and 80°34′ east longitude. To the north-east, beyond the Ganga, the deep stream of which forms the boundary of

the district, lie the districts of Hardoi and Unnao, while to the south, across the Yamuna, are the districts of Hamirpur and Jalaun. On the south-east , the boundary marches with that of Bindki (a tahsil of Fatehpur) and to the west and north-west are the district Kanpur Dehat and that of Kannauj district.

Area

According to the Central Statistical Organization, the district has an area of 3015 sq.km (Census, 2001) with 1040 sq.km area covered under Kanpur district, from which four zones were selected for the present study.

Population

According to the Census of 2001, the district had a population of 25,51,337 in which 13,74,121 are males and 11,77,216 are females and occupied the 2nd position in the State in respect of population.

Climate

The climate of the district is characterized by a hot summer and general dryness except in the south-west monsoon season. The year may be divided into four seasons. The period from March to about the middle of June is the summer season, which is followed by the south-west monsoon season which lasts till about the end of September, October and the first half of November forms the post-monsoon or transition period. The cold season spreads from about the middle of November to February.

Rainfall

Records in rainfall in the district are available for 8 stations for periods ranging from 51 to 97 years. The average annual rainfall in the district is 778.9 mm (30.67″). The rainfall in the district varies from 642.3 mm (25.29″) at Narwal to 884.8

mm (34.83″) at Kanpur. About 89 per cent of the annual rainfall is received during the monsoon months (June to September). August being the rainiest month. The variation in the annual rainfall from year to year as appreciable. In the fifty-year period, 1901 to 1950, the highest rainfall, which was 155 per cent of the normal, occurred in 1904. The lowest annual rainfall, 43 per cent of the normal, occurred in 1981. Ion this fifty-year period, the annual rainfall in the district was less than 80 per cent of the normal in 12 years, none of which were consecutive.

Temperature

There is a meteorological observatory at Kanpur and the record of this observatory may be taken as representative of the climatic conditions prevailing in the district in general. About the beginning of March there is a rapid rise in temperature. May and the early part of June constitute the hottest part of the year. The mean daily maximum temperature in May is 41.3°C (106°F) or above. Hot dry and dust leaden westerly winds are common in the hot season. Afternoon thunder showers that occur a few times during the summer, bring temporary relief, with the onset of monsoon after the middle of June, the day temperature drops appreciably. Nights continue to be as warm as those during the latter part of the summer. Towards the end of the monsoon (in September and in October) there is a slight increase in the day temperature, but the nights temperatures decrease rapidly. January ion generally the coldest month with the mean daily maximum temperature at 22.3°C (72.1°F) and the mean daily minimum at 7.8°C (46.0°F). During the cold season, in association with passing western disturbances, cold weaves affect the district and the minimum temperature drops down to about the freezing point of water and frost occurs. The highest maximum and the lowest maximum temperature recorded in the year 1996-97 and 1997-98 were 44.2°C and 0.7°C, respectively.

Humidity

During the monsoon season, the humidity generally exceeds 70 per cent but after that is decreases. The driest part of the year is the summer season when in the afternoon the humidity is less than 30 per cent.

Selected Sample of Kanpur City

Kanpur is well developed city. Kanpur city divided in different zones. Out of this four zones selected in this study. 60 respondents were selected form each zone. Thus, total 240 respondents were selected in the study area.

Research Methodology

This chapter deals with the research procedures applied in conducting the present study. For convenience, the research methodology has been discussed under the following three sub-heads :

1. Research design;
2. Variables and their Operationalization; and
3. Data gathering procedure and statistical techniques used.

1. Research Design

It comprises of the following sub-parts :

(*i*) Locale of the study;

(*ii*) District under study;

(*iii*) Selection of the area;

(*iv*) Sample of respondents;

(*v*) Pilot study; and

(*vi*) Pre-testing of instruments.

Locale of the Study

Uttar Pradesh was chosen as locale of the study. This was done with the intension that U.P. is a major State of the country.

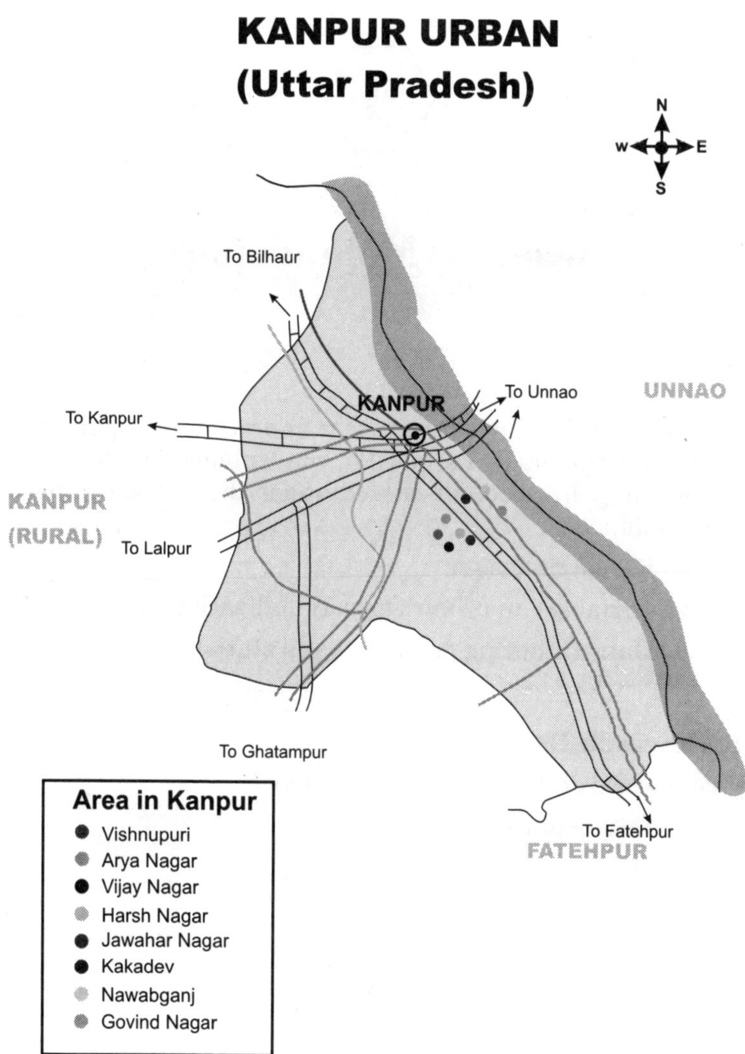

Fig. 4.1. Kanpur Urban (Uttar Pradesh)

District under Study

District Kanpur was purposively selected for this study as the researchers hailed from this place. This helped the investigator to collect the necessary information accurately and timely. The researcher, being from the same place could easily have dialogues and discussions with respondents during pilot study and final data collection.

Selection of the Area

District Kanpur comprises of different zones. Out of which four zones were randomly selected.

Selection of Respondents

A list of male and female were prepared separately for each zone. Male and female both were selected randomly from each. Thus, in all 240 respondents male (150) and female (90) were selected for study purpose.

Pilot Study

Prior to finally deciding the title of the project a pilot survey of the area was conducted. This gave an idea about the place of the study and nature of the samples that could be drawn and type of aspects and problems, which could be explored out.

Pre-testing of Instruments

Before collecting the necessary data from the finally selected sample of 240 male and female were identified other than those included in the final sample of respondents. These 240 respondents were interviewed with the help of schedules and questionnaires developed for collecting the data. This helped the investigator in making necessary changes in the instruments to be finally used their wording and composition.

Variables and Their Measurements

Independent Variables

(a) Age : The chronological age of respondents at the time of investigation was taken. All males and females were

listed according to following age groups and given the scores as follows (Table 4.1) :

Table 4.1. Age

Age-group (years)	Score assigned
(*a*) 20 – 30	1
(*b*) 30 – 40	2
(*c*) 40 – 50	3
(*d*) 50 onwards	4

(b) Educational qualification : Education was operationalized as the number of years of formal education obtained by the respondents. Scores assigned to different categories (Table 4.2).

Table 4.2. Educational Qualifications

Educational qualification	Score assigned
High school	1
Intermediate	2
Graduate	3
Post-graduate & above	4

(c) Sex : The sex of respondents at the time of investigation was taken. All respondents were listed according to sex and given the scores as follows (Table 4.3) :

Table 4.3. Sex

Sex	Score assigned
Male	1
Female	2

(d) Caste : Caste of the respondents in the study was measured on the basis of response of individual to which they belong, *i.e.* in terms of upper caste, backward caste and

schedule caste/schedule tribe. The scores were assigned in Table 4.4.

Table 4.4. Caste

Caste	Score assigned
General	1
Other backward caste (OBC)	2
Schedule caste/Scheduled tribe (SC/ST)	3

(e) Religion : The selected area was having mostly Hindu religion and some are Muslims. The following scoring pattern was adopted (Table 4.5).

Table 4.5. Religion

Category	Score assigned
Hindu	1
Muslim	2
Sikh	3
Christian	4

(f) Economic status : This was measured on the basis of the scores allotted to different family's economic status (Table 4.6).

Table 4.6. Economic Status

Economic status	Score assigned
Lower class	1
Middle class	2
Upper class	3

(g) Income : This was measured on the basis of the scores allotted to different family's income in the socio-economic status scale (Table 4.7).

Table 4.7. Income

Income	Score assigned
Up to Rs. 10,000	1
Rs. 10,000 to Rs. 20,000	2
Rs. 20,000 to Rs. 30,000	3
Rs. 30,000 and above	4

(h) Social participation : This was measured on the basis of the scores allotted to different family's social participation (Table 4.8).

Table 4.8. Social Participation

Caste	Score assigned
Member of 1 - 2 organization	1
Member of 3 - 4 organization	2
Member of 5 & more organization	3

Dependent Variables

Affair : A romantic and emotionally intense sexual or emotional relationship that may not last long that is between two people who are not married to each other.

Relationship : A state involving mutual dealings between people or parties or countries state – the way something is with respect to its main attributes.

Opinion : An opinion is a person's idea and thoughts towards something. It is an assessment, judgment or evaluation of something. An opinion is not a fact, because opinions are not falsifiable, or the opinion has not been proven or verified. If it later becomes proven or verified, it is no longer an opinion, but a fact.

Constraint : Explicit limitations that will be encountered in pursuing an objective. Examples of constraints are limitations in machine capacity, necessary materials or skilled labour.

Psychological Stress : Psychological stress is more to do with the turning of the body's stress responses to a situation. Psychological stress may have evolved from a real event that causes an emotional disturbance in the past. This event may have been the messy, splitting up from a relationship that leads to emotional pain.

Gender : Sexual identity especially is relation to society or culture. Traditionally, gender has been used primarily to refer to the grammatical categories of masculine, feminine and neuter, but in recent years the world has become well established in its use to refer to sex-based categories.

Community : A group of people living in the same locality and under the same governments. It is a group of people having common interests.

Effect : Something that produces a specific impression or supports a general design or intention.

Cause : Events that provide the generative force that is the origin of something.

Reason : The capacity for rational thought or interference or discrimination, an explanation of the cause of some phenomenon.

Invitation : A request (spoken or written) to participate or be present or take part in something, a tempting allurement.

Extra-marital Relations : Extra-marital affair is defined as an ongoing physical (sexual) relationship of a married person with an outsider (someone other than their own wife or husband). In some societies, an extra-marital affair may also consider as non-sexual but an extreme emotional attachment to an outsider. Some individuals may have an extra-marital affair with multiple partners. Since individuals who get into an extra-marital affair cannot enjoy it in open public with the fear of getting caught, there is a high sense of negligence anyway. There are cases one person is simply taking advantage of the other and nothing more.

Construction of Interview Schedule

The schedule for the present investigation was thus developed in accordance with the methodological procedure described above, keeping in view the objectives of the investigation.

Data Collection

The necessary evidences were collected in line with the objectives of the study. All the 240 respondents were inclusively approaches by the researcher. By personal contact, all the respondents were interviewed with the help of the structured schedule developed for the study.

Period of Investigation

The data collection was initiated from September 2008 to April, 2009.

Statistical Analysis

The following statistical techniques have been applied in the analysis of data.

1. Percentage : Single comparisons were made on the basis of the percentage, for drawing percentages, the frequency of a particular cell was multiplied by 100 and divided by total number of respondents in that particular category to which they belonged.

$$\text{Percentage} = \frac{\text{The sum of all the responses}}{\text{Total number of all the responses}} \times 100$$

2. Chi-square Test : In order to test the independence of two attributes a Chi-square test was applied as—

$$\chi^2 = \sum_{i=1}^{n} \frac{(o_i - E_i)^2}{E_i}$$

Where,

o_i = Observed frequency of ith cell

E_i = Expected frequency of ith cell

In $r \times c$ contingency table, χ^2 value is compared at $(r-1) \times (c-1)$ degree of freedom with theoretical value of χ^2 at 5 per cent level of significance.

3. Weighted Mean : All the items are not of equal importance. At the time they are given proper weights according to their relative importance, and then the average which is calculated on the basis of these weight is called weighed average of the weighted mean.

$$\text{Weighted mean} = \frac{W_1X_1 + W_2X_2 + W_3X_3 + \ldots W_nX_n}{W_1 + W_2 + W_3 \ldots W_n}$$

$$= \sum_{i=1}^{n} \frac{W_iX_i}{W_i}$$

4. Correlation Coefficient : Karl Pearson has given a coefficient of correlation for the measurement of linear relationship, which exists between two variables. If X and Y are two variables and if $E(X,Y) \neq 0$ then correlation coefficient (r) is

$$r = \frac{\text{Cov.}(X, Y)}{\sqrt{\text{Var.}(X)\,\text{Var.}(Y)}}$$

or

$$= \frac{\Sigma xy}{\sqrt{\Sigma x^2 \cdot \Sigma y^2}}$$

where,

$$\Sigma xy = \left[\Sigma XY - \frac{\Sigma X\, \Sigma Y}{n}\right]$$

$$\Sigma x^2 = \left[\Sigma X^2 - \frac{(\Sigma X)^2}{n}\right]$$

$$\Sigma y^2 = \left[\Sigma Y^2 - \frac{(\Sigma Y)^2}{n}\right]$$

and n = Sample size.

Here, one variable is dependent on other. For testing the significance of correlation coefficient (r), t test is applied. Degree of lack of relationship or coefficient of alienation is measured as–

$$K = \sqrt{1-r^2}\ .$$

Findings and Discussion

The empirical results and its discussion have been presented in this chapter. For the purpose of convenience, the findings of the study have been sub-divided under the following heads :

I. Socio-economic status of male and female.

II. Opinion of gender discrimination about extra-marital relations.

III. Assess the advantages and disadvantages of extra-marital relations

IV. Psychological stress of extra-marital relationship.

V. Constraints of extra-marital relations to maintain in future.

SOCIO-ECONOMIC STATUS OF MALE AND FEMALE

For the vast majority of male interviewees, issues of socio-economic status, specifically the intersection of economic and gender inequality, featured in accounts of their extra-marital relationships. Most often a man's relationship to his female lover included an expectation that the man provide certain kinds of economic support. Men frequently view extra-marital

relationships as arenas for the expression of economic and masculine status. Indeed, it is necessary to understand the intertwining of masculinity and wealth and gender and economics more generally, to make sense of the most common forms of extra-marital sexual relationships.

Age

Table 5.1 and Fig. 5.1 reveal the distribution of respondents according to age, maximum 38.7 per cent male belonged to 40 to 50 years age group whereas, 30 per cent male respondents belonged to 30 to 40 years age group, 41.1 per cent female respondents belong to 30 to 40 years age-group. 23.3 per cent female respondents belonged to 20 to 30 years age-group. Majority of male respondents (68.7%) belonged to middle age group (30 to 50 years). Age-group plays an important role in extra-marital relationship. "Human Relations" a complex yet interesting part in life.

Table 5.1. Distribution of respondents according to age

Age group (years)	Male	Female	Total
20 – 30	27 (18.0)	21 (23.3)	48 (20.0)
30 – 40	45 (30.0)	37 (41.1)	82 (34.2)
40 – 50	58 (38.7)	20 (22.2)	78 (32.5)
50 onwards	20 (13.3)	12 (13.4)	32 (13.3)
Total	150 (100.0)	90 (100.0)	240 (100.0)
χ^2		7.316	P > 0.05

Figures in parentheses indicate percentage of respective values.

Age is an important factor in having extra-marital relationship. According to psychologists after 40 years, there is a psychological change occur in males that why extra-marital relation usually occur.

Up to 40 years males are settled in family life means get married and generally financially more stable and strong.

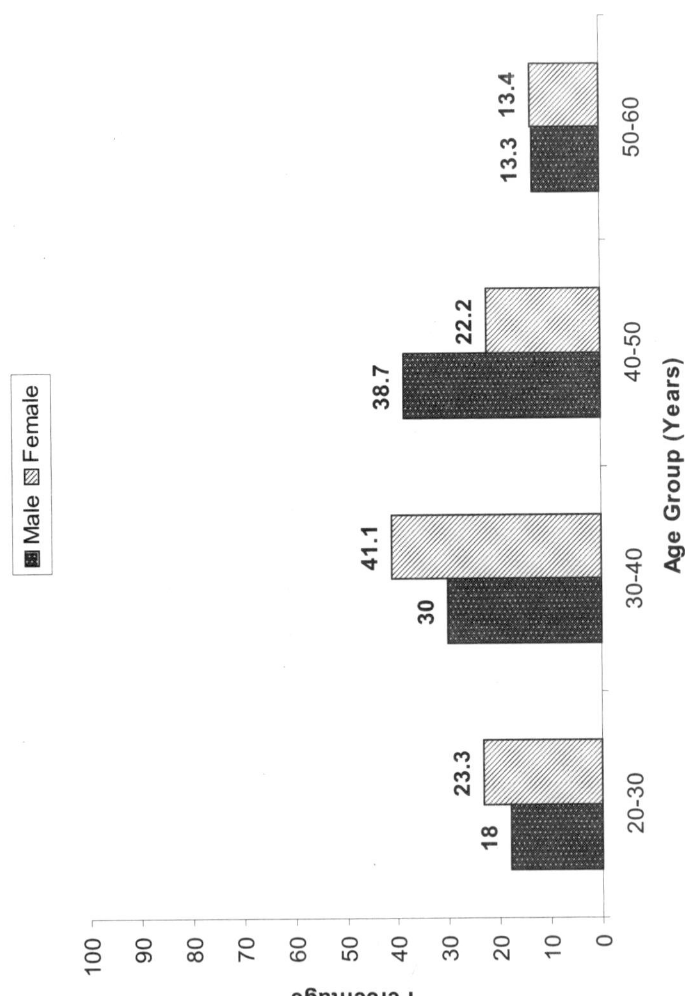

Fig. 5.1. Distribution of respondents according to age group

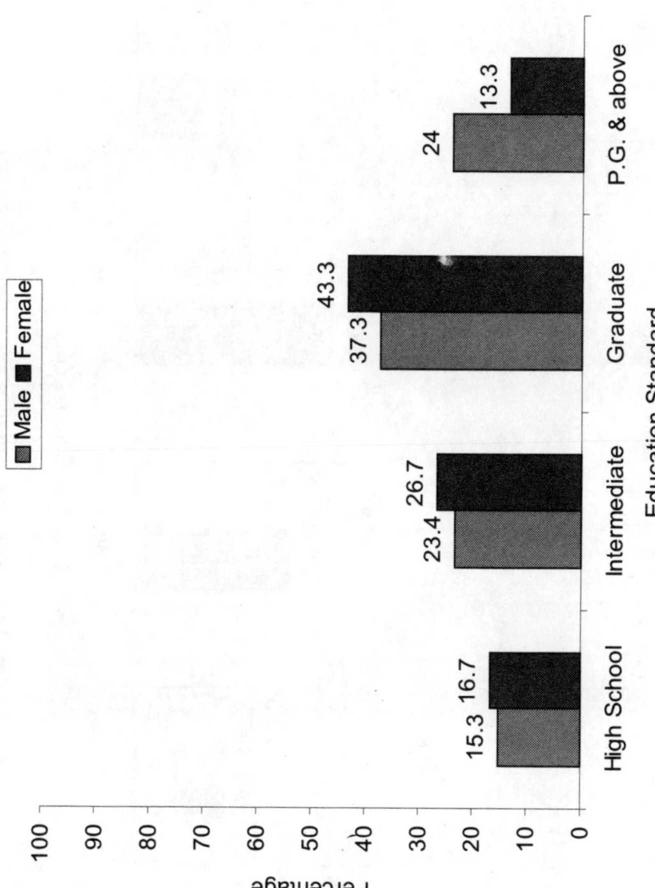

Fig. 5.2. Distribution of respondents according to education

Feels sometime relaxation towards responsibility so due to relaxed situations, economically strong conditions males attract towards EMR. The value of χ^2 was non-significant at five per cent level of significance.

Education

The perusal of Table 5.2 and Fig. 5.2 reveals the distribution of respondents according to education, 37.3 per cent male respondents were educated up to graduate level whereas 24.0 per cent PG and above. 43.3 per cent female respondents were educated up to graduate level whereas 26.7 per cent female respondents have passed Intermediate. 39.6 per cent respondents have passed graduate and 20.0 per cent respondents have passed PG and above. Married men having affairs with married women is less common, though its frequency varies depending on the couple's social class.

Table 5.2. Distribution of respondents according to education

Education	Male	Female	Total
High School	23 (15.3)	15 (16.7)	38 (15.8)
Intermediate	35 (23.4)	24 (26.7)	59 (25.6)
Graduate	56 (37.3)	39 (43.3)	95 (39.6)
PG & above	36 (24.0)	12 (13.3)	48 (20.0)
Total	150 (100.0)	90 (100.0)	240 (100.0)
χ^2		4.029	$P > 0.05$

Figures in parentheses indicate percentage of respective values.

For married men, the pretty urban educated young women who are the most desirable girlfriends provide not only sex but also the opportunity or at least the fantasy, of having more exciting, stylish, and modern sex than what they have with their wives. Married men who have younger girl-friends assert a brand of masculinity wherein sexual prowess, economic capability, and modern sensibility are intertwined.

Only education is not responsible for extra-marital relations. Because since ancient time in lower strata of society, lack of education extra-marital relation still persist in this strata. They develop extra-marital relations with their close or distant relatives. But in modern society males and females both are educated and also develop these relationship. Extra-marital relations persist generally in society. The observed value of χ^2 was non-significant at 5 per cent level of significance.

Sex

Table 5.3 and Fig. 5.3 show the distribution of respondents according to sex, 62.5 per cent male respondents and 37.5 per cent female respondents. Marital relationship are related to sex of the respondents are disharmony in married life, proximity at work place, high expectations from marriage, extended periods away form home, loneliness and depression, fulfilling a sexual fantasy, physical attraction, prolonged dating and sexual intimacy of people is common cause of developing extra-marital relationship. Extra-marital relationship were strongly influenced by the gender of the married individual.

Table 5.3. Distribution of respondents according to sex

Sex	Frequency	Per cent
Male	150	62.5
Female	90	37.5
Total	240	100.0

There are some gender differences in how men and women view extra-marital relationships, although these are generalizations, not true in every instance. Women seem to be drawn into adulterous relationships initially through emotional attachments, while men are more likely attracted sexually. Interestingly, each gender tends to assume that

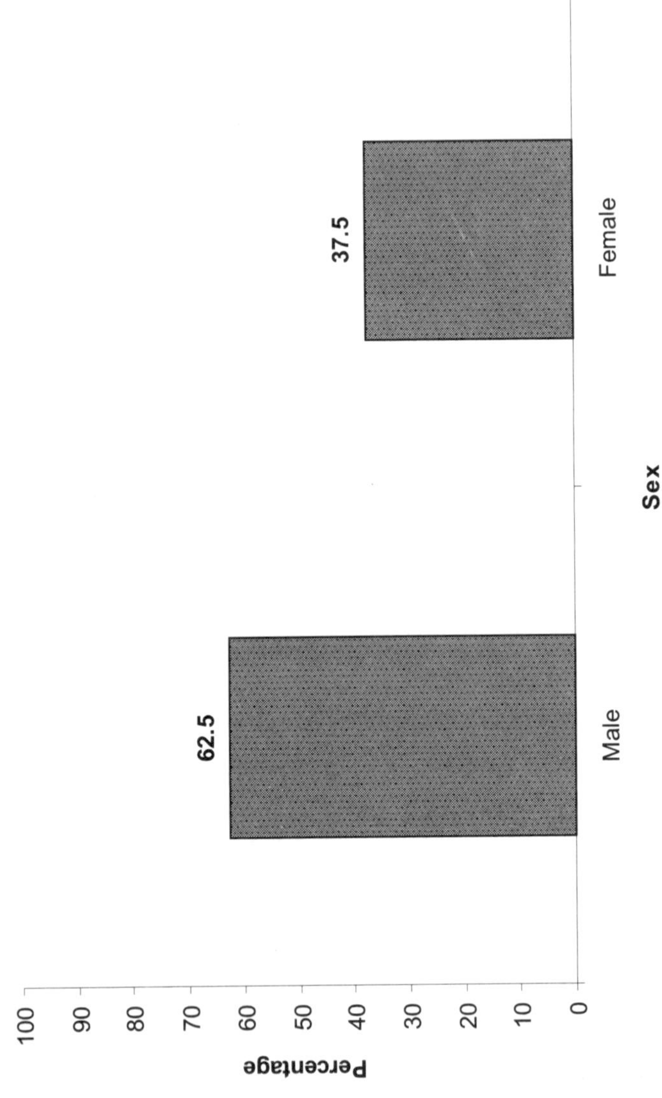

Fig. 5.3. Distribution of respondents according to sex

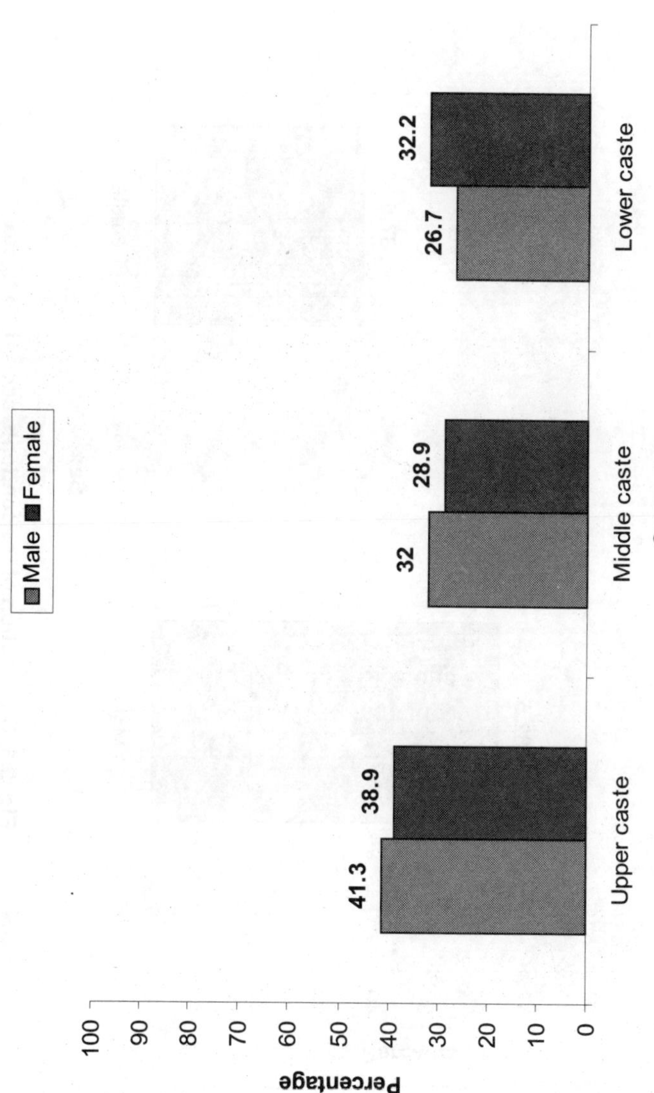

Fig. 5.4. Distribution of respondents according to caste

the other is acting out of the same motivation as they are likely to themselves. Women assume that their husband has become emotionally attached to another woman, when his interest may be primarily physical, Men make the mistake of thinking that their wife's relationship with another man is safe if she shows no physical attraction to him. These issues may need to be addressed in the recovery process in order that both husband and wife can understand the development of extra-marital relationship.

Caste

Table 5.4 and Fig. 5.4 show the distribution of respondents according to caste, 41.3 per cent male respondents belonged to upper caste whereas 32 per cent middle caste. 38.9 per cent female respondents belonged to upper caste whereas 32.2 per cent respondents were of lower category. Majority of 40.4 per cent respondents belonged to upper caste whereas 30.8 per cent belonged to middle category. Caste plays an important role in extra-marital relations of the respondents. Extra-marital affairs can cause a ripple effect in life. People may find themselves looking differently at their job, their friends and their life choices. The observed value of χ^2 was significant at 5.0 per cent level of significance.

Table 5.4. Distribution of respondents according to caste

Caste	Male	Female	Total
Upper caste	62 (41.3)	35 (38.9)	97 (40.4)
Middle caste	48 (32.0)	26 (28.9)	74 (30.8)
Lower caste	40 (26.7)	29 (32.2)	69 (28.8)
Total	150 (100.0)	90 (100.0)	240 (100.0)
χ^2		0.864*	P > 0.05

Figures in parentheses indicate percentage of respective values.

Religion

Table 5.5 and Fig. 5.5 indicates that 52.0 per cent male respondents belonged Hindu religion whereas 22.7 per cent male respondents belonged Muslim religion. 52.2 per cent female respondents belonged to Hindu religion whereas 23.3 per cent female belonged Christian. More than fifty five per cent respondents belonged Hindu family while 17.9 per cent belonged to Muslim family. Minimum 12.5 per cent respondents belonged to Sikh religion. Extra-marital affairs be the result of an inability to maintain a satisfying emotional relationship with a partner over a long period of time. The observed value of χ^2 (8.273*) was significant at 5 per cent level of significance.

Table 5.5. Distribution of respondents according to religion

Caste	Male	Female	Total
Hindu	78 (52.0)	47 (52.2)	125 (52.1)
Muslim	34 (22.7)	9 (10.0)	43 (17.9)
Christian	21 (14.0)	21 (23.3)	42 (17.5)
Sikh	17 (11.3)	13 (14.5)	30 (12.5)
Total	150 (100.0)	90 (100.0)	240 (100.0)
χ^2		8.273*	$P < 0.05$

Figures in parentheses indicate percentage of respective values.

Monthly Income

Table 5.6 shows the distribution of respondents as per monthly income, 29.3 per cent male respondents have earned Rs. 30,000 and above, whereas 32.7 per cent male respondents have earned Rs. 10,000 to Rs. 20,000 monthly. 37.8 per cent female respondents have earned Rs. 20,000 to Rs. 30,000 monthly while 25.6 per cent female respondents have earned Rs. 30,000 and above monthly. 27.9 per cent respondents have earned Rs. 30,000 and above monthly followed 28.3 per cent respondents have earned Rs. 20,000 to Rs. 30,000 monthly. Minimum 14.6 per cent respondents have earned up to Rs. 10,000 monthly. The calculated value of χ^2 (6.655) was non-significant at 5 per cent level of significance.

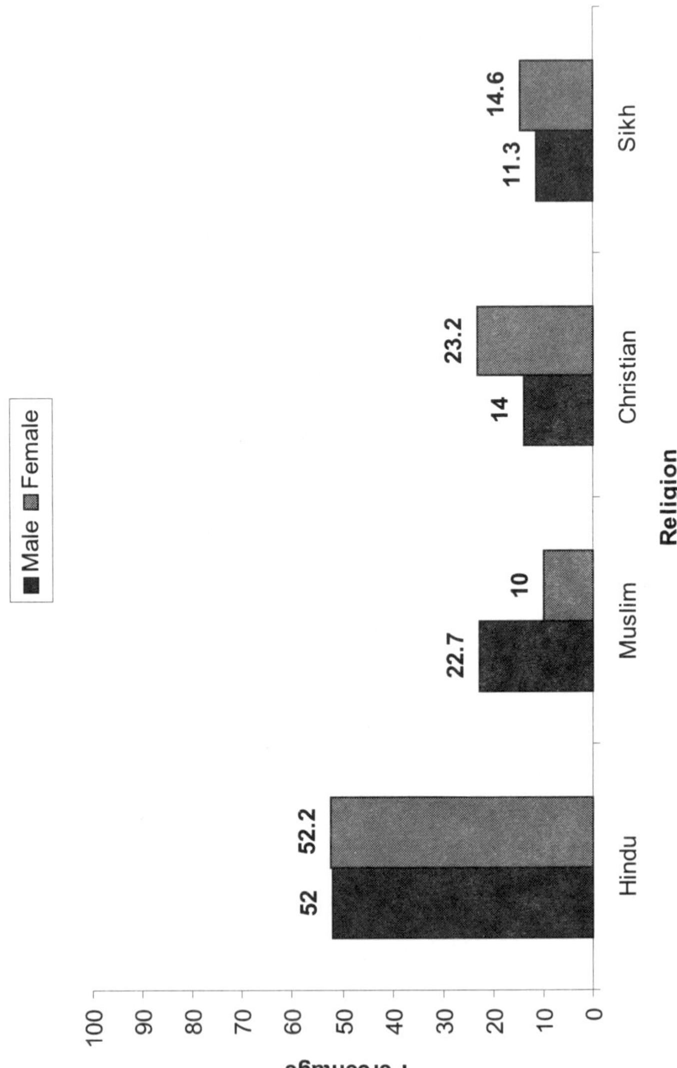

Fig. 5.5. Distribution of respondents according to religion

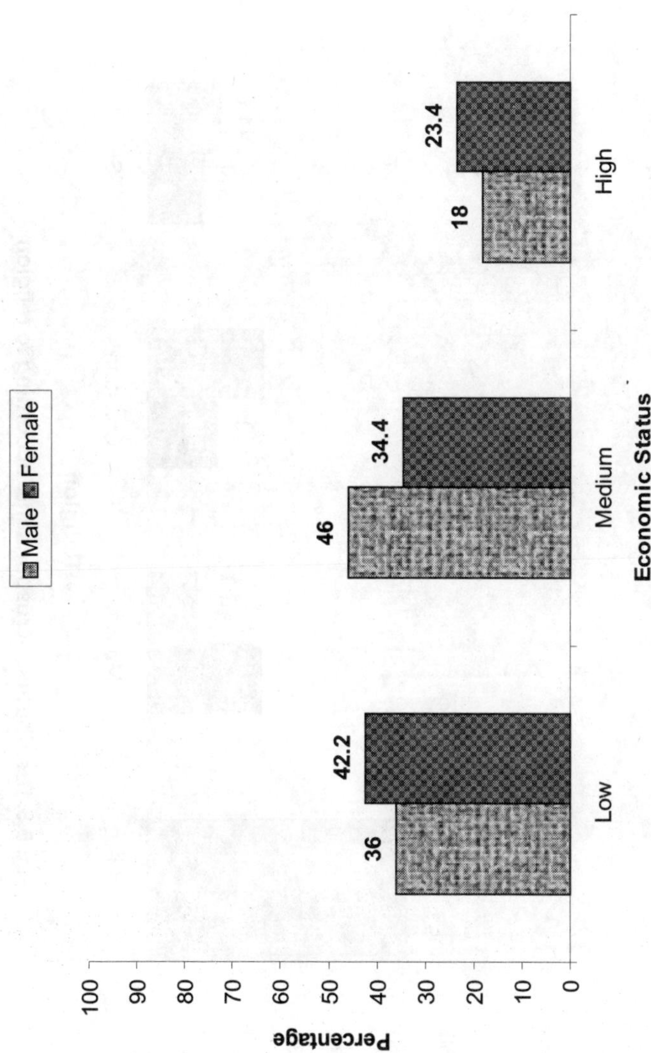

Fig. 5.6. Distribution of respondents according to religion

Table 5.6. Distribution of respondents as per monthly income

Income (in Rs.)	Male	Female	Total
Up to Rs. 10,000	23 (15.3)	12 (13.3)	35 (14.6)
Rs. 10,000 to Rs. 20,000	49 (32.7)	21 (23.3)	70 (29.2)
Rs. 20,000 to Rs. 30,000	34 (22.7)	34 (37.8)	68 (28.3)
Rs. 30,000 & above	44 (29.3	23 (25.6)	67 (27.9)
Total	150 (100.0)	90 (100.0)	240 (100.0)
χ^2		6.655	P > 0.05

Figures in parentheses indicate percentage of respective values.

Economic Status

Table 5.7 and Fig. 5.6 show that distribution of respondents according to economic status, 18 per cent male belonged to high economic status whereas 46 per cent have medium economic status. 23.4 per cent female respondents belonged to high economic status while 34.4 per cent female have medium economic status. Minimum (42.2%) female respondents were from low economic status family. Overall 20.0 per cent respondents have high, 41.7 per cent medium and 38.3 per cent have low economic status.

Table 5.7. Distribution of respondents according to economic status

Economic status	Male	Female	Total
Low	54 (36.0)	38 (42.2)	92 (38.3)
Medium	69 (46.0)	31 (34.4)	100 (41.7)
High	27 (18.0)	21 (23.4)	48 (20.0)
Total	150 (100.0)	90 (100.0)	240(100.0)
χ^2		3.171	P > 0.05

Figures in parentheses indicate percentage of respective values.

It is clear that men with money have easier access to end, it seems, more frequent extra-marital sex. But poorer

men engage in extra-marital sex as well, and their relationships with female partners also typically include some form of transaction, whether it is paying a sex worker or giving gifts to a girlfriend, albeit at a lower financial level than that of more elite men. Although there is no doubt that the desire to forge and present a modern masculine identity combines issues of economics and gender, not all men's extra-marital relationships can be easily explained in these terms.

Economic status is an important factor in having extra-marital relations. Extra-marital have more commonly shown in high and low economic status people. Because in high economic status, people have lots of money so their mind divert toward pleasure, enjoy and fashion. For pleasure people engage in wife-swapping e.g., doctor, businessman, politician etc. In low economic status due to crisis of money their full enjoyment depends around family. So for money, husband involves her wives in promiscuity that is the reason of extra-marital relation in low economic status. Only in medium economic status due to pressure of family and fear people have few extra-marital relations.

Social Participation

Table 5.8 reveals the distribution of respondents according to social participation, maximum more than forty per cent male respondents have participated and member of 3 to 4 organizations whereas, 29.3 per cent male respondents have member of 1 to 2 organizations. 46.7 per cent female respondents have a member of 3 to 4 organizations, whereas, 34.4 per cent female respondents have joined 1 to 2 organizations. Minimum 22.9 per cent respondents have joined 5 and more organization. Every human living in structured social groups, human have adhered to the belief that formal unions of two people work best for maintaining a healthy functioning society. Human being have been engaging in non-monogamous activities throughout history.

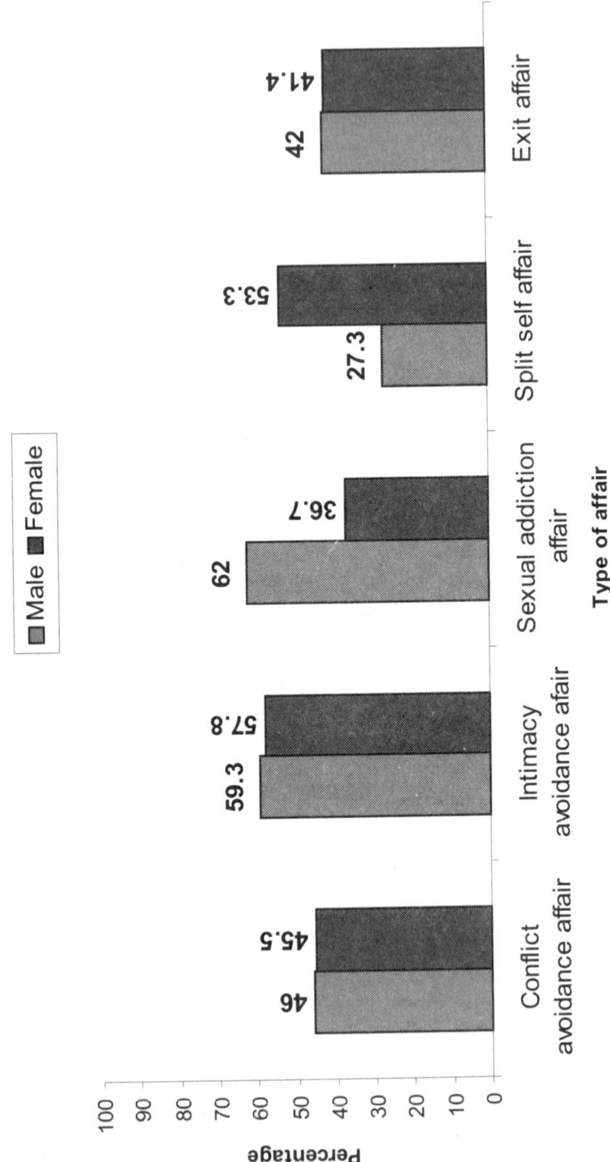

Fig. 5.7. Distribution of respondents in extra-marital relationship

Table 5.8. Distribution of respondents according to social participation (organisation)

Social participation	Male	Female	Total
Member of 1-2 organizations	44 (29.3)	31 (34.4)	75 (31.3)
Member of 3-4 organizations	68 (45.3)	42 (46.7)	110 (45.8)
Member of 5 & more organizations	38 (25.4)	17 (18.9)	55 (22.9)
Total	150 (100.0)	90 (100.0)	240 (100.0)
χ^2		1.511	$P > 0.05$

Figures in parentheses indicate percentage of respective values.

Masculinity is created and expressed both in men's relationships to women and in their relationships with other men. In male-dominated social settings such as social clubs, sports clubs, sections of the marketplace, and particular bars and eateries, Igbo men commonly talk about their girlfriends and sometimes show them off. Male peer groups are a significant factor in many men's motivations for and behaviours in extra-marital relationships.

OPINIONS OF GENDER DISCRIMINATION ABOUT EXTRA-MARITAL RELATIONS

Table 5.9 and Fig. 5.7 reveal the types of affair according to male and female in extra-marital relationship. 62.0 per cent male and 36.7 per cent female have desired sexual addiction affair, sexual addicts use sex over and over again to numb inner pair and emptiness much like alcoholics use alcohol. Among married people, men are sexual addicts more often than women. 59.3 per cent male and 57.8 per cent female were showed intimacy avoidance affair are frightened of getting too close, so they keep the barriers high between them. Conflict is one barrier, affair is another. Their emotional connection with each other is through frequent and intense conflict. These couples are the mirror opposite of

Table 5.9. Type of affair according to male and female in extra-marital relationship

Type of affair	Male		Female		χ^2
	Yes	No	Yes	No	
Conflict avoidance affair	69 (46.0)	81 (54.0)	41 (45.5)	49 (54.5)	0.013
Intimacy avoidance affair	89 (59.3)	61 (40.7)	52 (57.8)	38 (42.2)	0.056
Sexual addiction affair	93 (62.0)	57 (38.0)	33 (36.7)	57 (63.3)	14.476*
Split self affair	41 (27.3)	109 (72.7)	48 (53.3)	42 (46.7)	16.298*
Exit affair	63 (42.0)	87 (58.0)	37 (41.1)	53 (58.9)	0.018

(Figures in parenthesis indicate percentage of respective values)

the conflict avoiders. 46.0 per cent male and 45.5 per cent female were showed conflict avoidance affairs where they can't resolve their difference and the marriage erodes. 27.3 per cent male and 53.3 per cent female have split self affair tried to do marriage right. Both spouses have sacrificed their own feelings and needs to take care of others, and the deprivation has caught up with one of them. The affairs are serious, long-term and passionate. The spouse who is having affair focuses on deciding between the marriage and the affair partner and avoids looking at the inner split. Only 42.0 per cent male and 41.1 per cent female were engaged in exit affair where in one spouse has already decided to leave the marriage and the affair provides the justification. Quite often one partner has emotionally divorced over a long period of time even though the couples are still living together. This is sometimes called equal opportunity affair.

Table 5.10 reveals that extra-marital opinion according to time duration, 24.0 per cent male respondents engaged more than one month towards attraction and 14.7 per cent male were engaged more than one year duration in friendship towards female. 28.7 per cent male have engaged up to 30 days in sexual relationship and 12.0 per cent male were involved more than one year in sexual relationship. 3.3 per

cent female respondents were engaged in up to 30 days in attraction towards males whereas 23.3 per cent female were attracted for more than one month. 20.0 per cent female have attract towards male in friendship more than one month. 3.3 per cent female have taking sexual relationship up to one month whereas 17.8 per cent female have engaged in sexual relationship to male more than one month.

Table 5.10. Extra-marital relationship according to time duration

Relationship	Male			Female		
	Up to one month	More than one month	More than one year	Up to one month	More than one month	More than one year
Attraction	22 (14.7)	36 (24.0)	92 (61.3)	3 (3.3)	21 (23.3)	66 (73.3)
Friendship	29 (19.3)	22 (14.7)	99 (66.0)	4 (4.4)	18 (20.0)	68 (75.5)
Sexual relationship	43 (28.7)	89 (59.3)	18 (12.0)	3 (3.3)	16 (17.8)	71 (78.9)

Figures in parentheses indicate percentage of respective values.

Main factors for development of extra-marital relationships are work place, stage shows, co-education, professional carriers etc. Due to carrier orientation, higher education, now-a-days there are so many males and females who are adopting single hood. Due to single hood it is natural to attract towards opposite sex. Females are emotionally weak so they generally emotionally attract towards married or even unmarried males. In married women when husband is not paying attention towards them. They also develop extra-marital relations. In elite class and in lower strata of society like slums there is 40 per cent married women who are involved in extra-marital relations.

The perusal of Table 5.11 and Fig. 5.8 reveal that opinion of male and female of extra-marital relationship, 74.0 per cent male and 74.4 per cent female have taking relationship as a fashion/status symbol whereas 70.7 per cent male and 52.2 per cent female were suffered disharmony in married life.

Table 5.11. Opinion of gender discrimination about extra-marital relations

Opinion	Male	Female
Attraction	94 (62.7)	41 (45.5)
Friendship	70 (46.7)	50 (55.5)
Increased employment of women	36 (24.0)	72 (80.0)
Disharmony in married life	106 (70.7)	47 (52.2)
Fashion/status symbol	111 (74.0)	67 (74.4)
Unsatisfaction from sexual relations	87 (58.0)	32 (35.5)
Lack of love	48 (32.0)	29 (32.2)
Family stress		
(*i*) Economic	21 (14.0)	46 (51.1)
(*ii*) Long period of illness	12 (8.0)	36 (40.0)
(*iii*) Job tension	26 (17.3)	53 (58.9)
r	0.089	

(Figures in parenthesis indicate percentage of respective values)

62.7 per cent male and 45.5 per cent female respondents were attracted towards opposite sex while 58.0 per cent male and 35.5 per cent female were unsatisfied from sexual relations, sex is perhaps one of the most important reasons why troubles start in relationships. Sex is an amalgamation of love and passion between two people. With time sex can become monotonous and if there is a lack of desire, passion and romance in the relationship then it may drive the person to seek it with someone else. Many people do not seem to be bothered about their actions or what effects their behaviors may have on the others. Consequently it has become socially acceptable and not entirely unusual for people to say that they weren't happy and this is the reason many give in having extra-marital affairs. 32.0 per cent male and 32.2 per cent female have suffered lack of love in married life, love like other emotions changes with time. The initial

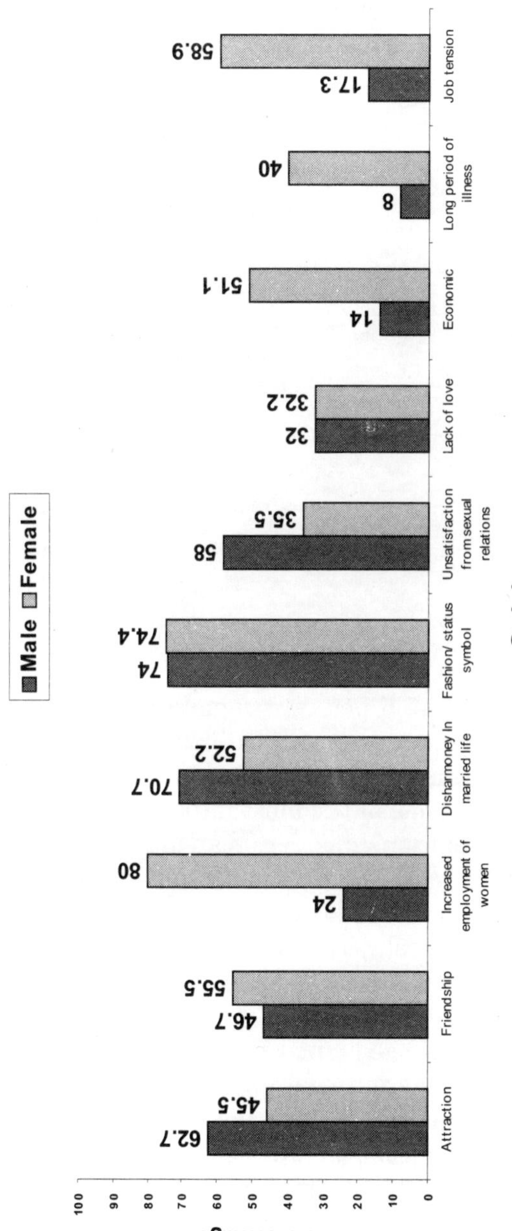

Fig. 5.8. Opinion of gender discrimination about extra marital relations

excitement and adrenalin of the first few years fades away with the passage of time. Sometimes people find it difficult to deal with this problem as they believe they need the excitement, passion and love rekindled. 17.3 per cent male and 58.9 per cent female were suffering job tension whereas 51.1 per cent female and 14.0 per cent male have economic problem, remove these type of stress they link with other opposite sex relationships to satisfy their sexual needs and orgasms such romance and sex addicts are usually driven by the passion they find in new relationships.

In an study on extra-marital relationship, as per the opinion of male and female, the first preference was attraction. Second chance of friendship was working together. 80 per cent males opined that in family life due to less interest in sex and lack of romantic love with wife they get attracted with opposite sex. Ten years after marriage, responsibility takes place in place of attraction in male and female. Due to which there is more chances of increasing extra-marital relations in males. But in females the increase in extra-marital relations are due to domestic violence, irritating activity, ignorance and embarrassment by their counterparts.

Table 5.12 shows that causes of extra-marital affairs of respondents, 50.7 per cent male and 72.2 female have given causes as dispute marriage itself is damaged or the relations between the two people are neglected and strained then it can result in people having affairs. Finances, sharing, intimacy, religion are all important issues. Many marriage experience conflicts and if the individuals are not equipped to resolve the conflicts then it can cause problems and in the light of these problems one of the partner may be tempted to seek happiness and satisfaction elsewhere. 42.0 per cent male and 56.7 per cent female have reasons self-esteem problem and such individuals are not able to handle the usual problems in the relationship. They are also often driven by the need to feel loved because of their low self-esteem and search for companionship and love in person other than their

Table 5.12. Causes of extra-marital affairs

Causes of extra-marital affairs	Male		Female		χ^2
	Yes	No	Yes	No	
Dispute marriage	76 (50.7)	74 (49.3)	65 (72.2)	25 (27.8)	10.785*
Enjoyment	84 (56.0)	66 (44.0)	31 (34.4)	59 (65.6)	10.430*
Self-esteem problem	63 (42.0)	87 (58.0)	51 (56.7)	39 (43.3)	4.852*
Lack of love	88 (58.7)	62 (41.3)	35 (38.9)	54 (60.0)	8.307*
Psychological changes in man	80 (53.3)	70 (46.7)	—	—	0.667
Difference of age in partner	67 (44.7)	83 (55.3)	54 (60.0)	36 (40.0)	5.290*
Unsatisfaction of sex	69 (46.0)	81 (54.0)	63 (70.0)	27 (30.0)	13.091*
Sex curiosity	98 (65.3)	52 (34.7)	39 (43.3)	51 (56.7)	11.113*
Desire for happiness	82 (54.7)	68 (45.3)	56 (62.2)	34 (37.8)	1.314
Less commitment	26 (17.3)	124 (82.7)	41 (45.6)	49 (54.4)	22.264*
Unrealistic expectation	33 (22.0)	117 (78.0)	46 (51.1)	44 (48.9)	21.588*
Inability to cope with cultural ethnic differences	24 (16.0)	126 (84.0)	40 (44.4)	50 (55.6)	23.273*
Disappointment that one partner has not grown in the same way	76 (50.7)	74 (49.3)	14 (15.6)	76 (84.4)	29.587*

Figures in parentheses indicate percentage of respective values.

partner. Both of the male and female causes significantly dependent on self-esteem problem. 54.7 per cent male and 62.2 per cent female have desire for happiness, as the society progresses selfishness and an individualistic pattern of

thinking has become the norm. Relationship have also become quite dispensable for some people. The observed value of χ^2 was not significant at 5.0 per cent level of significance. 56.0 per cent male and 34.4 per cent female were enjoying extra-marital affairs. The observed value of χ^2 (10.430*) was significant at 5.0 per cent at 1 d.f. While 44.7 per cent male and 60.0 per cent female were engaged in extra-marital relationship due to difference of age in partner. 53.3 per cent male respondents have engaged in sexual relationship due to psychological change in man according to their age. 46.0 per cent male and 70.0 per cent female were engaged in extra-marital relations due to unsatisfied of sex, this is the very common problem now-a-days. The value of χ^2 (13.091*) was significant at 5.0 per cent at 1 d.f. 17.3 per cent male and 45.6 per cent female have causes less commitment, many individuals have commitment problems and often find it easier to walk out when the going gets tough. Changed attitudes towards life have also reduced the commitment levels and importance of the institution of marriage. Education and career have taken precedence in many cases and people are not as committed towards marriage. The observed value of χ^2 (22.264*) was significant at 5.0 per cent level of significance, commitment associated with sex. 22.0 per cent male and 51.1 per cent female have showed unrealistic expectations reasons in relationships, many individuals get married with a lot of unrealistic expectations from their partners. The problem in this case is not with the relationship itself but with the believes and ideas about the relationship, many people are not equipped to accept and handle that the initial euphoria subsides. If one of the individuals in a marital relationship is not mature enough to handle the changes in the relationship then he or she may opt for an extra-marital affairs. The observed value of χ^2 (21.588*) was significant at 5.0 per cent level of significance hence unrealistic expectation associated with sex. 65.3 per cent male and 43.3 per cent female have given reason sex whereas 52.0 per cent male and 54.4 per cent female

were given love as a causes of extra-marital relationships to seek love, companionship outside the marriage include mid life crisis. Sexual abstinence is also one of the effects of extra-marital affairs. It will be very difficult for the individual to experience any degree of security and faith in the relationship again. One third of men and one fifth of women are deeply engaged in extra-marital intercourse. Men are more willing than women to have sex with someone they have known for a day or less, but women prefer to know someone for a longer period before becoming intimate. When the marriage is experiencing problems and during those times one partners turn towards a friend or companion of the opposite sex. 50.7 per cent male and 15.6 per cent female have disappointment that one partner hasn't grown in the same way, women seen to be drawn into adulterous relationships initially through emotional attachments while men are more likely attracted sexually. One person feels ignores in the relationship and just for sometime needs to be away from the tension and pressure. 16.0 per cent male and 44.4 per cent female have inability to cope with cultural or ethnic differences in their sex drive and in the sex drive of their partner, one partner withhold sex or shows little interest the other partner may fill that need outside the marriage. The loss of the high level of passion and desire that existed in the beginning of the relationship may result in boredom or develop into a feeling of apathy towards the partner.

The causes of extra-marital affairs have been many as well as varied. Some have been frivolous, a little branch from critical matrimony problems as well as a little come from low mental problems. It can be astray to connect all people in an event with a same brush usually as it is not a great thought to proceed any event with a same attitude.

Most affairs we might think, branch from problems with a matrimony though in being usually a little of those affairs have been without delay associated to problems of marriage. People with low self venerate as well as certainty mostly rush problems in a matrimony since they cannot hoop them, they

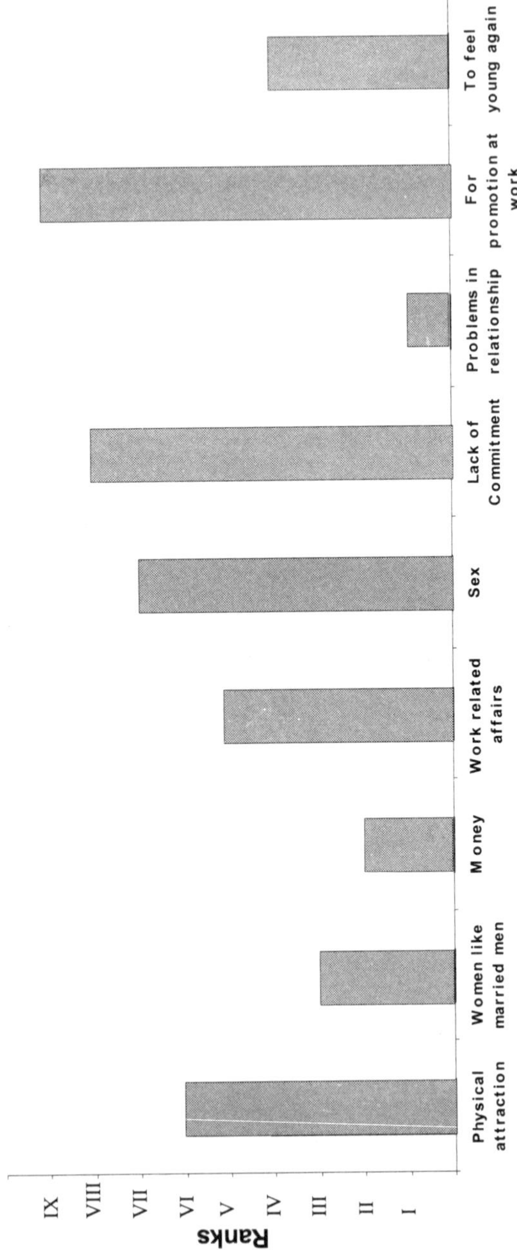

Fig. 5.9. Powerful reason due to which women engage in extra-marital affairs

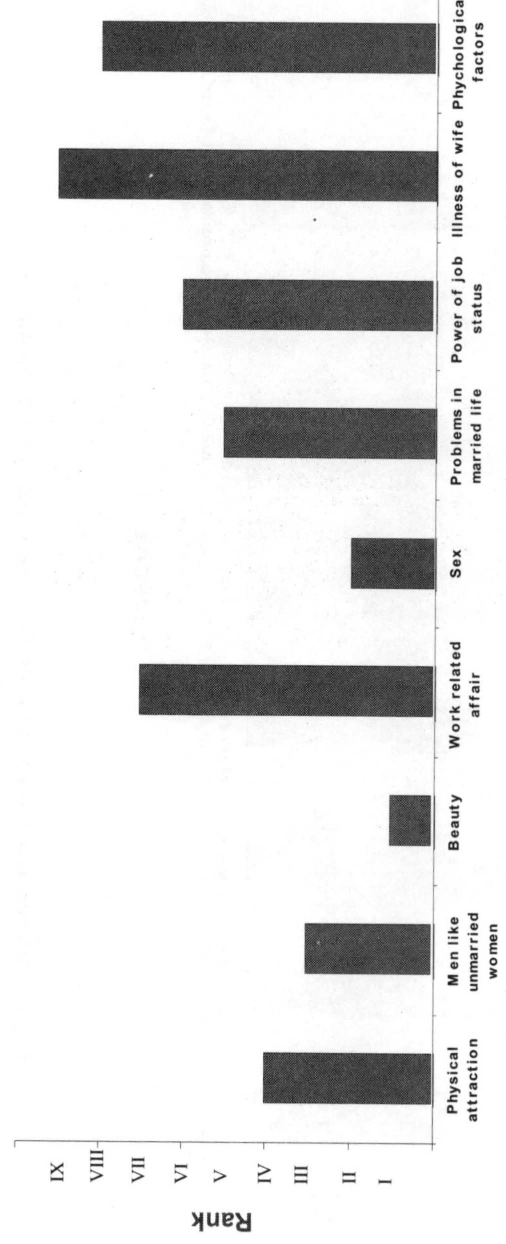

Fig. 5.10. Powerful reasons due to which men engage in extra-material affairs

can additionally spin to alternative people for adore since they feel homely or unloved as well as find which out in others rather than operative on it with their spouse. This can infrequently be the hardest complaint to repair since it is a mental need of your partner which needs to be marinated as well as if it is not treated with colour can resurface again as well as again.

As many as people wish to hold adore is a psychic thing, which transcends many relations with troubles equates to issues for men as well as women alike. Love as well as matrimony is not a single aspect though an alliance of things as well as is a vital part of it. Without enterprise as well as passion a rest of a relationship can be poisoned. Misunderstandings about a significance of in between men as well as women can mangle marriages as well as expostulate people to an affair. While troubles might be caused by alternative problems in a relationship it is mostly a many viewable starting indicate to demeanour at fixing.

Table 5.13 and Fig. 5.9 reveal that powerful reasons of extra-marital affairs of women, 76.7 per cent women have attract towards many in extra-marital affair because the other person is rich and they can enjoy many things in life which they otherwise cannot afford. 81.1 per cent female respondents have feel problems in relationship, this may be frequent arguments with current life partner or could be stress over children. 62.2 per cent female like married men because women are emotional and they often feel married men can understand their feelings much better in comparison to the bachelors. 45.5 per cent female respondents have no proper healthy atmosphere for work related affairs, they engaged in any personal relationship with coworkers and spend a majority of time at work and even though her initial dates may start with simply personal problems the relationships can easily get intense with time. 21.1 per cent women may engaged in a relationship for promotion or for a raise in her life.

Table 5.13. Powerful reasons due to which women engage in extra-marital affairs

Reasons	Female respondents			
	Yes	No	Scores	Rank
Physical attraction	37 (41.1)	53 (58.9)	1.41	VI
Women like married men	56 (62.2)	34 (37.8)	1.62	III
Money	69 (76.7)	21 (23.3)	1.77	II
Work related affairs	41 (45.5)	49 (54.4)	1.45	V
Sex	31 (34.4)	59 (65.5)	1.34	VII
Lack of commitment	26 (28.9)	64 (71.1)	1.29	VIII
Problem in relationship	73 (81.1)	17 (18.9)	1.81	I
For promotion at work	19 (21.1)	71 (78.9)	1.21	IX
To feel young again	46 (51.1)	44 (48.9)	1.51	IV

Figures in parentheses indicate percentage of respective values.

Some women who have been a flirt before marriage may find it difficult to eventually commit to just one person. 34.4 per cent women find having sex with new partners as exciting and may fulfil their hidden fantasies. Sometimes women are forced into having an extra-marital affair due to blackmail or an unfair advantage by the other person.

The extra-marital affair is known as an ongoing physical relationship of a married person with an outsider. In some places the extra marital affairs also consider as the non-sexual relation but an extreme emotional attachment to an outsider.

Life is not perfect and therefore many women may not find the happiness in relationship with their life partner and attraction to an outsider with an exception that it will void that gap in their life, which has been created by the life partner. Sometime women are happily married and even have children may have extra-marital affairs just to spice up their life. There are many powerful reasons due to which women engage in extra-marital affairs. Physical attraction is the biggest reason why women cheat their life partner.

May be they loose attraction because their life partner has lost hair and several other reasons due to which they are no longer physically attracted towards her?

The perusal of Table 5.14 and Fig. 5.10 reveals that powerful reasons due to which men engaged in extra-marital affairs, 91.3 per cent men respondents were attract towards beauty of women, whereas 88.0 per cent male attract towards sex appeal of women. 81.3 per cent men always like unmarried young girl, because they attracted and wishes to have unwanted relationship. 52.0 per cent men have engaged in extra-marital affairs due to problems in married life loss of physical relationship between the couples they forget the fact that a good sexual life is essential for a healthy marital relationship. The continuous withdrawal from the sexual acts, prompts the other partners to seek the physical satisfaction from another source, which in turns leads to extra-marital affairs. 62.0 per cent men attracted towards physical attraction of women, the men who get into a love marriage often laments that, they had only seen the good

Table 5.14. Powerful reasons due to which men engaged in extra-marital affairs

Reasons	Female respondents			
	Yes	No	Scores	Rank
Physical attraction	93 (62.0)	57 (38.0)	1.62	IV
Men like unmarried women	122 (81.3)	28 (18.7)	1.81	III
Beauty	137 (91.3)	13 (8.7)	1.91	I
Work related affairs	69 (46.0)	81 (54.0)	1.46	VII
Sex appeal	132 (88.0)	18 (12.0)	1.88	II
Problems in married life	78 (52.0)	72 (48.0)	1.52	V
Power and job status	70 (46.7)	80 (53.3)	1.47	VI
Illness of wife	65 (43.3)	85 (56.7)	1.43	IX
Psychological factors	67 (44.7)	83 (55.3)	1.45	VIII

(Figures in parenthesis indicate percentage of respective values)

side of their partner prior to marriage. The over possessiveness and jealousy often couple them to turn their back against their chosen marriage and to seek a less complex marital life. 46.7 per cent men wanted extra-marital affairs due to power and job status while 43.3 per cent men wanted other relations due to illness of his wife in sex or other diseases in body the situations becomes worse as they do not receive due support from their partners, they may find an outsource to cry out their dilemmas, who may better understood the true feelings thus person engaged in sexual activity with someone other than their marriage partner.

In India an arranged marriage signifies the marriage between two families at many times the prospective couple find it very difficult to adjust with the norms and culture of the other one's family.

Table 5.15 and Fig. 5.11 reveal that distribution of male and female according to invitation of extra-marital

Table 5.15. Invitation of extra-marital relationships by male and females

Invitation	Male	Female
Disharmony in married life	129 (86.0)	69 (76.7)
Proximity at the workplace	62 (41.3)	44 (48.9)
High expectations from marriage	66 (44.0)	29 (32.2)
Change in circumstances	64 (42.7)	43 (47.8)
Loss of passion	54 (36.0)	36 (40.0)
Extended periods away from home	72 (48.0)	59 (65.5)
Loneliness and depression	81 (54.0)	66 (73.3)
Fulfilling a sexual fantasy	108 (72.0)	41 (45.5)
Revival of an old flame	71 (47.3)	12 (13.3)
Physical attraction	82 (54.7)	38 (42.2)
r	0.688*	

Figures in parentheses indicate percentage of respective values.

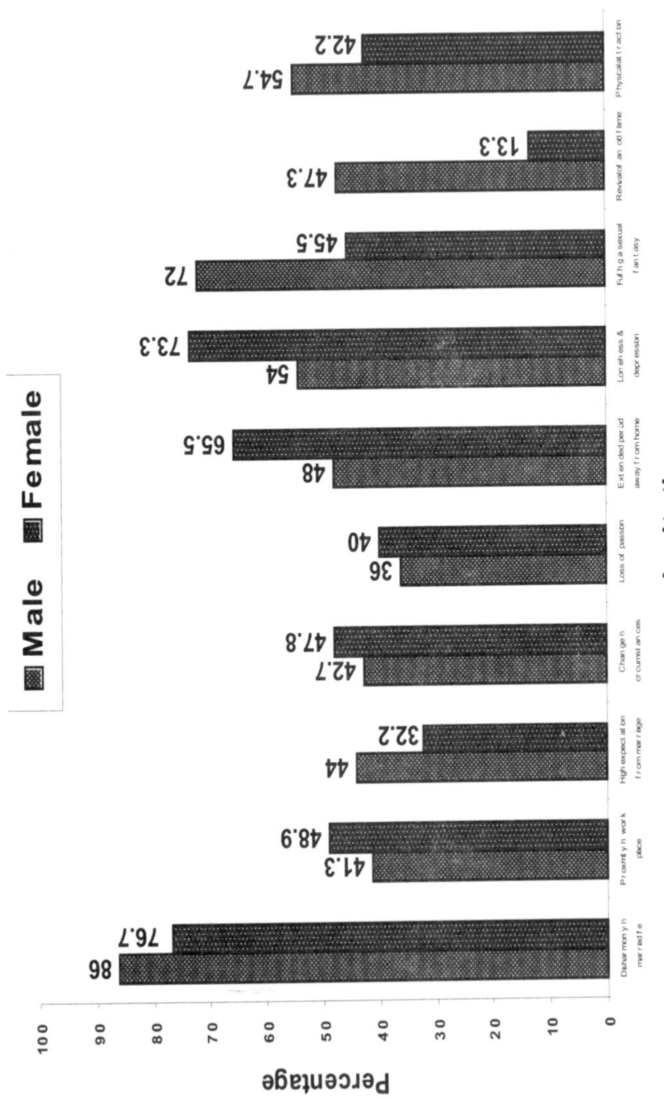

Fig. 5.11. Invitation of extra-marital relationships by respondents

relationship, 86.0 per cent male and 76.7 per cent female have suffered disharmony in married life whereas 72.0 per cent male and 45.5 per cent female were invite extra-marital relationship for fulfilling a sexual fantasy. 54.7 per cent male and 42.2 per cent female have attracted towards physical looking whereas 47.3 per cent male and only 13.3 per cent female were used relationship for revival of an old flame. 48 per cent male and 65.5 per cent female were engaged extra-marital relationship who lived long periods away from home. This factor operates in cases where the husband/wife has to be frequently away on business tours or to attend conferences or is forced to stay away from the spouse due to the place of work being distant. Sexual desire is one of the strongest physiological drives may be due to the biological need. A lousy sex life means that unfulfilled sexual desires keep accumulating and ultimately the frustrated man or woman looks for a outlet. This outlet is often found in a colleague or a close relative. The proclivity towards having an affair is a symptom of an individual's inability to find satisfaction in a long-term relationship because of the high expectations placed on the relationship or the spouse initially. A man or woman who is successful a celebrity and much admired becomes a target for the opposite sex. A substantial number of people end up having extra-marital relations due to sheer physical attraction. The fundamental force for sex is the sexual desire, especially if, the earlier relationship included sex that was fulfilling and enjoyable more like a sex worker selling herself, there are times when favours multiply and the temptation is too great.

The commonest cause for a disturbed family environment is an unsatisfactory sex life. Other causes are incompatibility between partners, financial problems and all-too-common social problems like the "in-law" syndrome. In such situations, the person seeks some solace outside the marriage. Proximity at the workplace is probably the commonest factor—especially in urban settings. In recent years, a flood of women have joined the workforce, either to start their own business,

fulfil their own ambitions or seek economic independence. This trend is obviously increasing as the pressure of enhancing the family income grow. Increasing as the pressure of enhancing the family income grow. Increasing female literacy is providing more work opportunities. What this has done is facilitate contact between male and female colleagues, in many causes in a one-on-one situation or at least in close proximity to each other. Mutual attraction is a logical and natural occurrence. To begin with, the physical virtues of a colleague are responsible for this though it is often camouflaged with the façade of intellectual compatibility. Infatuations like this ultimately lead to the bedroom.

Obviously, colleagues with troubled married lives are more susceptible. However, in quite a few cases, it starts off with oversexed males looking for a fling. Beware the male who says he is just looking for a shoulder to weep on because of differences with his wife. The search for solace and sympathy is, coincidentally, always directed at single women. It's an age-old ploy and it is surprising how many well-educated, highly intelligent women fall into this trap.

Some people find it difficult if not impossible to remain 'in love' with their partners as they grow older are mature. This 'falling out of love' can lead to the search for a new sexual partner or a different sexual experience. The sudden change in circumstance provides an incentive for some people to look for another intimate relationship or multiple sex partners. The loss of the high level of passion and desire that first attracted two people to each other can over a period of time, drift into boredom and develop into a feeling of apathy towards the partner. Combined with all the other stresses and complexities of long-term relationships – financial problems, raising demand of children, job changes, changes in status loss of position – it may lead to a desire to rediscover lost passion in the arms of someone new. These are the periods which make a person emotionally weak and vulnerable. A helping hand or a shoulder to weep on if

available in such times can create a situation of intimacy and lead to the initiation of an extra-marital relationship. Obviously in these situations, both the partners are quite willing and if they enjoy the experience, then the possibility of a longer-term relationship exists. Very often this happens between a middle aged, married male and a young, unmarried woman. Physical factors are the primary force in such scenarios.

ADVANTAGE AND DISADVANTAGE OF EXTRA-MARITAL RELATIONS

Table 5.16 shows that advantages of extra-marital relationship, 52.7 per cent male were given opinion maintain personality whereas 46.7 per cent female respondents maintain personality in extra-marital relationship. The calculated value of χ^2 (0.810) was non-significant at 5.0 per

Table 5.16. Advantages of extra-marital relationship

Advantages	Male		Female		χ^2
	Yes	No	Yes	No	
Become more attractive	79 (52.7)	71 (47.3)	42 (46.7)	48 (53.3)	0.810
Enthusiasm towards work	64 (42.7)	86 (57.3)	29 (32.2)	61 (67.8)	2.585
To look younger	98 (65.3)	52 (34.7)	46 (51.1)	44 (48.9)	4.741*
Increase liveliness	110 (73.3)	40 (26.7)	63 (70.0)	27 (30.0)	0.311
Decreasing stress	76 (50.7)	74 (49.3)	34 (37.8)	56 (62.2)	3.864*
More sincere towards family	43 (28.7)	107 (71.3)	43 (47.8)	47 (52.2)	8.935*
Isolation decreases	89 (59.3)	61 (40.7)	54 (60.0)	36 (40.0)	0.010
Reduce health hazard	58 (38.7)	92 (61.3)	38 (42.2)	52 (57.8)	0.296

Figures in parentheses indicate percentage of respective values.

cent, 1 d.f. conclude that both sex wants to maintain personality. 42.7 per cent male and 32.2 per cent female respondents increase their work efficiency due to extra-marital relations. The observed value of χ^2 (2.585) was non-significant at 5 per cent level, 1 d.f. 65.3 per cent male respondents look younger while 51.1 per cent female respondents have look younger due to extra-marital relations. The observed value of χ^2 (4.741*) was significant at 5 per cent conclude that both sex (male and female) wants become looks younger. 73.3 per cent male respondents have believed in living and 70 per cent female have believed in living whatever they wants they do. 50.7 per cent male and 37.8 per cent female have reduced stress when they engaged opposite sex friendship and extra-marital relationship. In opposite sex relations they feel happy. The observed value of χ^2 (3.864*) was significant at 5.0 per cent and 1 d.f. hence male and female both are reduced stress in extra-marital relationship. 28.7 per cent male and 47.8 per cent female have feel more caring in extra-marital relations. 59.3 per cent male and 60.0 per cent female were reduced loneliness with the help of extra-marital relations. The observed value of χ^2 (0.010) was non-significant. 38.7 per cent male and 42.2 per cent female have reduced health hazard in extra-marital relations.

Due to extra-marital relations, there is advantage also. Whenever any person attracts towards other there is feeling of looking better or smarter, which increases liveliness in the people. Due to enthusiasm feeling of affection, health hazards like blood pressure, stress, depression etc. reduces.

Extra-marital relations are a part of our culture. From Bill Clinton to the family next door, extra-marital affairs leave a trail of destruction and upheaval in the lives of everyday people. While the aftermath of an affair poses a sizable threat to the integrity of the relationship, an extra-marital relation does not always signify the end of a marriage. Patience, love, and understanding can work through the damage. However, it takes a lasting commitment on the part

of both people to sustain positive healing in the relationship. More often than not, one of the parties is not a willing participant in mending the relationship. Faith, friends, and a strong resolve can help in treading water until both parties can being working on rebuilding the lost bonds.

Table 5.17 shows that disadvantages of extra-marital relationship 50.0 per cent female have feeling insecure due to environment and society culture. 66.0 per cent male respondents have feel sexual transmitted diseases like HIV/ AIDS whereas 47.8 per cent female respondents feared catching a sexually transmitted disease. The observed value of χ^2 (7.731*) was significant at 1 d.f. and 5.0 per cent level of significance. The risk of sexually transmitted disease can be greatly reduced by practicing safer sex. Over 67.4 per cent male said that they had changed their behaviours because of the AIDS scare. A majority of respondents reported changing their behaviours in response to HIV/AIDS, some choose to become more selective in choosing partners rather than adopting safer sex practices. Many people are not aware they are infected and non outwards signs of infection may be visible.

Table 5.17. Disadvantages of extra-marital relationship

Disadvantages	Male		Female		χ^2
	Yes	No	Yes	No	
Feeling of insecurity in women	—	—	45 (50.0)	45 (50.0)	—
Fear of venereal diseases	99 (66.0)	51 (34.0)	43 (47.8)	47 (52.2)	7.731*
Ripple effect in life	121 (80.7)	29 (19.3)	56 (62.2)	34 (37.8)	9.885*
Social fear	46 (30.7)	104 (69.3)	37 (41.1)	53 (58.9)	2.712
Mental insecurity in women	—	—	63 (70.0)	27 (30.0)	—
Fear of conceiving	—	—	82 (91.1)	8 (8.9)	—

Psychological study suggests people may not be particularly good at detecting lies about HIV status. 80.7 per cent male respondents have given ripple effect in life whereas 62.2 per cent female respondents have given ripple effect in life, extra-marital affairs can cause a ripple effect in life, this can be either positive or negative, but most respondents of an affair say that it brought on changes in all other areas of their lives. Perhaps half of the adults suffering from severe stress blame the deteriorating relationships on their spouse. Looking at the growing rate of divorces, court cases for alimony, physical abuses and single parents, it does seem as if handling a relationship can be a tricky and often taxing issue. The possible causes of stress can be endless such as—an unaffectionate spouse, unforgiving attitude of a spouse, handling of monetary affairs (budgeting, investments, expenditures), lack of proper communication between spouses, unable to find quality time for each other, extra-marital relationships, step children and dealing with in-laws. More often than not, stress arising from marital relationships is manifested in chronic disorders such as depression, insomnia and hypertension. Since a relationship depends on the nature of the persons involved, it helps to seek the middle path when the inherent individual differences surface. The breakdown of a relationship is one of our most stressful life events. One may lose his/her lover, friend, confidence and perhaps sense of self and direction. This is a time of extreme and mixed emotions made more complicated by stresses and worries about legal and financial considerations. People cope with their emotions in different ways, some people choose to ignore how they feel and carry on as if nothing has happened. The observed value of χ^2 (9.885*) was significant at 5 per cent level of significance conclude that both sex (male and female) have dependent to ripple effect in life. 30.7 per cent male have fear about extra-marital relationship whereas 41.1 per cent female have fear about relationship hence less relationship. The calculated value of χ^2 (2.712) was non-significant at 5.0 per cent level of significance. 70.0 per cent female respondents were feel

mental insecurity and 91.1 per cent female feels unwanted pregnancy due to extra-marital relations.

In females there is greater chance of disadvantages. Females feel mentally insecure if their partner is married because they know very well that there is no chance of marriage without divorce. In males they have fear of their family pressures, social pressure also.

Table 5.18 reveals that distribution of respondents according to extra-marital effects, 46.0 per cent male were affected by damage of self-esteem whereas 61.1 per cent female respondents were effected due to self-esteem. 68.0 per cent male have lack of trust in extra-marital relation whereas 57.8 per cent female have faced lack of trust. 38.0 per cent male respondents have faced sense of instability

Table 5.18. Distribution of respondents according to extra-marital effects

Disadvantages	Male		Female		χ^2
	Yes	No	Yes	No	
Damage to self-esteem	69 (46.0)	81 (54.0)	55 (61.1)	35 (38.9)	5.143*
Luck of trust	102 (68.0)	48 (32.0)	52 (57.8)	38 (42.2)	2.556
Sense of instability	57 (38.0)	93 (62.0)	66 (73.3)	24 (26.7)	28.108*
Roller-coaster of emotions	93 (62.0)	57 (38.0)	82 (91.1)	8 (8.9)	24.139*
Loss of passion	72 (48.0)	78 (52.0)	63 (70.0)	27 (30.0)	11.063*
Mental insecurity	16 (10.7)	134 (89.3)	79 (87.8)	11 (12.2)	139.858*
Economic insecurity	98 (65.3)	52 (34.7)	13 (14.4)	77 (85.6)	58.597*
Social pressure	111 (74.0)	39 (26.0)	63 (70.0)	27 (30.0)	0.451

Figures in parentheses indicate percentage of respective values.

whereas 73.3 per cent female have face sense of instability. 62.0 per cent male respondents have roller-coaster of emotion whereas 91.1 per cent female respondents have suffering in emotions in extra-marital relationships. 48.0 per cent male respondents have affected loss of passion due to psychological stress. Female have less loss of passion in comparison to male. Female have 87.8 per cent mental insecure, which is too high in comparison to male, 65.3 per cent male feel economic insecure due to expenditure of extra-marital relation. 70.0 per cent female and 74.0 per cent male have feel social pressure due to fear in extra-marital relationship.

The person who has been cheated on will suffer a below to his or her self-esteem. The victim of an affair will find it difficult to trust. He or she may doubt their judgment to others. Even if this relationship ends, and another begins, the baggage of infidelity can follow. Roller-coaster of emotions is common when faced infidelity to feel a myriad of emotions.

The effects of extra-marital affair on the relationship depend on the manner in which the couple approaches and attempts to resolve the problem. There will also be a deep resentment and anger towards the cheating partner. It will be very difficult for the individual to experience any degree of security and faith in the relationship again. Fear is also experienced as once an individual has had an affair his/her partner will remain fearful of such an event happening again. Sexual abstinence is also one of the effects of extra-marital affairs. This is because the spouse of the cheating individual may find it very difficult to allow the person to touch him/her after the fact of an affair is known.

Effect of an affair is the loss of trust. An affair will almost certainly destroy trust in marriage. In addition to the actual unfaithfulness, the affair may have, over time, also involved weeks or months of denial, dishonesty, secrecy, or other attempts to conceal an extra-marital relationship. If it is your spouse that had the affair, you may blame yourself for being the cause of it or that you were blind enough to have missed

the warning signs in the first place. Anger is another consequence of an extra-marital affair. A lot of people are angry after an affair, sometimes all throughout the remainder of their life.

Table 5.19. Effects of extra-marital relationship

Effects	Male	Female	Children	Home life
Mental stress	61 (40.7)	67 (74.4)	131 (54.6)	122 (50.8)
Loneliness	48 (32.0)	72 (80.0)	148 (61.7)	118 (49.2)
Economic status	92 (61.3)	39 (43.3)	23 (9.6)	81 (33.7)
Personality	79 (52.7)	42 (46.7)	69 (28.7)	—
Disgraceful	66 (44.0)	56 (62.2)	11 (4.6)	131 (54.6)

Figures in parentheses indicate percentage of respective values.

Table 5.19 and Fig. 5.12 indicate effect of extra-marital relationship, 40.7 per cent male and 74.4 per cent female were suffering mental stress whereas 32.0 per cent male and 80.0 per cent female have faced loneliness. 61.3 per cent male and 43.3 per cent female have used extra marital relationship due to economic status, whereas 52.7 per cent male and 46.7 per cent female were having dating in extra-marital relationship exhibit his or her personality. 61.7 per cent children have feels loneliness due to their parent's nature while 54.6 per cent children have faced mental stress due to loneliness and discarded by parents. 50.8 per cent whole family gone in mental stress. The indication is that the desire for a new sexual experience is not the initial motive for looking outside the marriage, but rather comes after the breakdown of the emotional relationship. Only then after there has been an eroding of the interpersonal relationship, including a loss of passion, lack of intimacy, and loss of emotional and sexual satisfaction does the dissatisfied partner look for a new lover to fulfill their needs. 54.6 per cent home life partners were running in disgraceful due to extra-marital relationship. A lousy sex life means that unfulfilled sexual

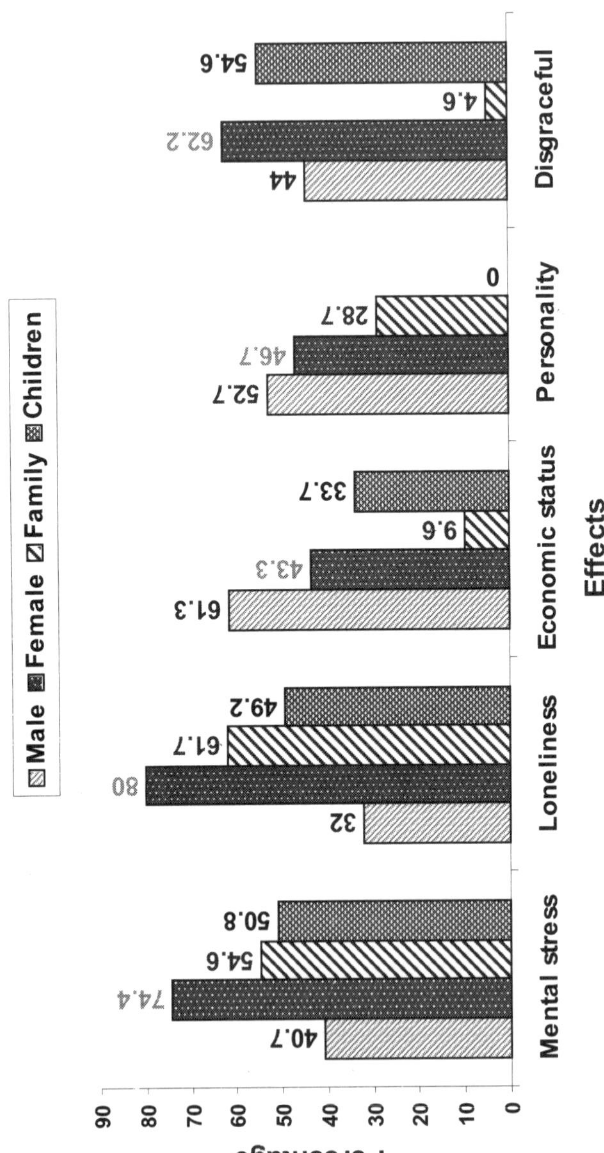

Fig. 5.12. Effects of extra-marital relationship

desires keep accumulating and ultimately, the frustrated man or woman looks for a outlet. Usually boils down to an urge to introduce variety in one's sex life.

Extra-marital relations are diverse but most often involve transferring of emotional energy that was once directed to the marital harmony and for the family and children to other sources such as career and outside interests and friends.

Actually, children's psychological reactions to their parents' divorce vary in degree dependent on three factors – (*i*) the quality of their relationship with each of their parents before the separation, (*ii*) the intensity and duration of the parental conflict, and (*iii*) the parents' ability to focus on the needs of children in their divorce.

Attachment theory of divorce : Children usually lose a degree of contact with one of their very few attachment figures when a divorce occurs. It is a confusing and stressful time for children, regardless of whether the divorce was amicable or not. Poor school performance, low self-esteem, behaviour problems, distress and adjustment difficulties are associated with divorce. In adolescents from divorced families they noted more instances of delinquent behaviour, early sex activity and continued academic issues. There are many factors that may play into how children's attachments are altered after a divorce, gender and age being the two most documented variables. It is also important to discuss the outcome of divorce and how it affects children's attachment style. Often times, divorces end in ugly custody battles between the parents. During this time the parents being terribly selfish as to who is most responsible often forget they are being observed at all times. Attachment style can be even more afflicted by court battles in which the child has no control over whom he or she goes with.

Due to increase in extra-marital relation in the society, the psychological problems are increasing day-by-day because our society has not accepted the extra-marital relation like in foreign countries. In male dominated society, there are more number of cases of extra marital relations in

males and they hide these relations with the society due to family fear and because of this they always feel guilt and remain live in depression. In Indian culture, unmarried human beings are mostly involved in extra-marital relation and this the reason for their depression and psychological problems. In females, mental insecurity and loneliness put them under problem because their partner is married. Unmarried girls must understand the limitations of having relations with married. This tops in chances of unhealthy relations.

PSYCHOLOGICAL STRESS OF EXTRA-MARITAL RELATIONSHIP

The perusal of Table 5.20 reveals that 37.3 per cent male and 64.4 per cent female have feels hypertension. χ^2 (16.579*) was significant 5 per cent and 1 d.f. hence male and female both feels hypertension. 48.0 per cent male and 81.1 per cent female have suffered depression in extra-marital relationship. The observed value of χ^2 (25.787*) was significant at 5.0 per cent level of significance. 46.0 per cent male and 47.8 per cent female respondents were feeling guilty in extra-marital relationship. Majority of the female

Table 5.20. Stress due to extra-marital relationships

Disadvantages	Male		Female		χ^2
Stress	Yes	No	Yes	No	
Hypertension	56 (37.3)	94 (62.7)	58 (64.4)	32 (35.6)	16.579*
Depression	72 (48.0)	78 (52.0)	73 (81.1)	17 (18.9)	25.787*
Guilty	69 (46.0)	81 (54.0)	43 (47.8)	47 (52.2)	0.071
Lack of manifest	17 (11.3)	133 (88.7)	51 (56.7)	39 (43.3)	56.930*
Lack of insomnia	71 (47.3)	79 (52.7)	16 (17.8)	74 (82.2)	21.262*
Mental insecurity	19 (12.7)	131 (87.3)	47 (52.2)	43 (47.8)	44.144*
Loneliness	86 (57.3)	64 (42.7)	53 (58.9)	37 (41.1)	0.056

Figures in parentheses indicate percentage of respective values.

respondents were feel lack of manifest and value of χ^2 (56.930*) was significant hence more women were faced lack of manifest. 11.3 per cent male and 56.7 per cent respondents have felt mentally insecure in extra-marital relationship. The observed value of χ^2 (21.262*) was significant at 5.0 per cent hence more than fifty per cent women have feel mental insecure compare to men. 57.3 per cent male and 58.9 per cent female respondents have taking stress towards loneliness in extra-marital relationship. The χ^2 value was non-significant at 5.0 per cent level of significance. The possible cause may be endless, but an unaffectionate and unforgiving attitude of spouse or extra-marital relationship on inability a quality time with spouse may cause stress.

The negative effect of deteriorating marital relationship will manifest as insomnia, hypertension and depression. The possible cause may be endless but an affectionate and unforgiving attitude of extra-marital relationship may cause stress.

The psychological stress due to extra-marital relations can be overcome in males and females for which they have to maintain limitations in their friendship. They have to make their relations open. There should not be over expectation. Because, when expectation is not fulfilled, it gets converted in stress. By making limitation in relation, the extra marital relations may continue long time in future. Together with love and affection, if one is caring, honest and responsible in understanding one another problems, there may not be a chance of stress. In extra marital relation, one should not be involved with more than one at a time. It helps in maintaining stability in relationship and their relations are arranged for long time.

Table 5.21 and Fig. 5.13 show that remove factors of psychological stress during extra-marital relationship, 62.0 per cent male were commitment for open relations whereas 74.4 per cent female were given same stress. 65.3 per cent male were given more than one relationship, generally male have wants to more relations in opposite sex to remove his

stress. Male does not want any expectation to his partner besides sexual relations so this is one cause to remove his stress. 92.2 per cent ladies have engaged in work herself to remove psychological stress and 84.4 per cent females do not have any expectations to her partner in sexual relations. 74.4 per cent female commit for open relations to remove her psychological stress.

Table 5.21. Remove of psychological stress

Remove stress	Male		Female	
	Fre- quency	Per cent	Fre- quency	Per cent
Commitment for open relations	93	62.0	67	74.4
No over expectations	36	24.0	76	84.4
Engage in work	48	32.0	83	92.2
More than one relationship	98	65.3	39	43.3
r		–0.7961		

Figures in parentheses indicate percentage of respective values.

For reducing the psychological stress there should be always open and fair relationship. There should be no over expectations. Mental insecurity, which may be generated due to betrayal, to reduce feeling of insecurity they may have more than one partner. The correlation coefficient between sex and stress was negative (–0.7961) at 5.0 per cent level of significance.

Table 5.22 shows that psychological stress of male according to economic status, 4.0 per cent male have low stress and high status while 10.7 per cent male have low stress and medium status. 20.7 per cent male have medium stress and medium status. 10.7 per cent male respondents have high stress and high status whereas 14.7 per cent male have high stress and medium status. 17.3 per cent male have high stress and low status. The observed value of χ^2 (2.378) was non-significant at 5.0 per cent and 4 d.f.

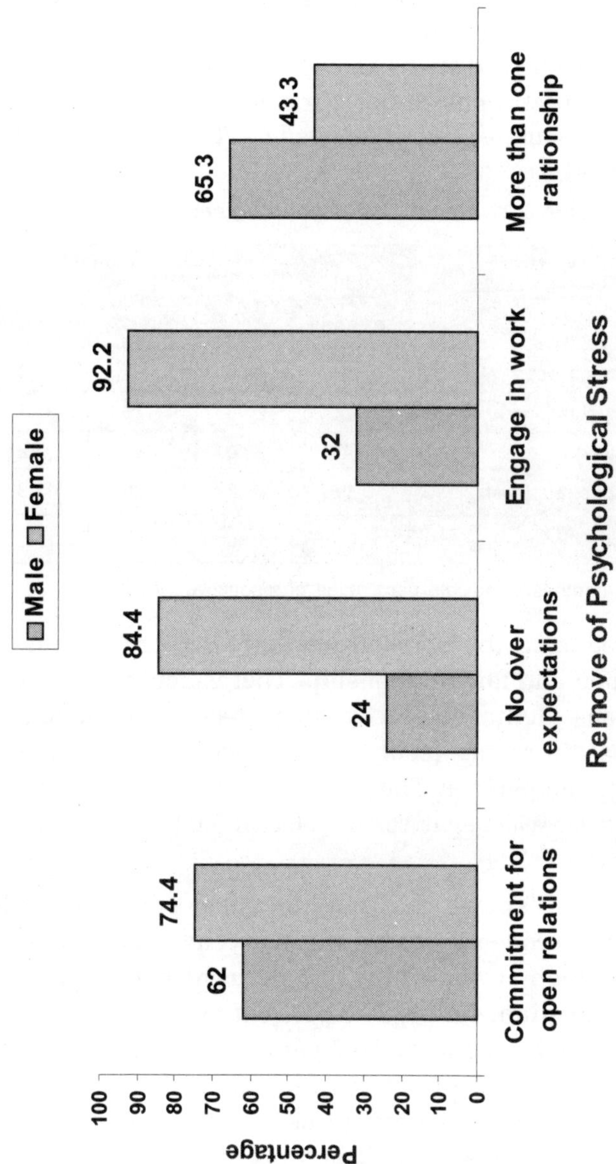

Fig. 5.13. Remove of Pychological Stress

Table 5.22. Psychological stress of male according to economic status

Economic status	Psychological stress		
	Low	Medium	High
Low	8 (5.3)	20 (13.3)	26 (17.3)
Medium	16 (10.7)	31 (20.7)	22 (14.7)
High	6 (4.0)	5 (3.3)	16 (10.7)
χ^2	2.378	P > 0.05	

(Figures in parenthesis indicate percentage of respective values)

Table 5.23 shows that psychological stress of female according to economic status, 6.7 per cent female have low stress and high status while 10.0 per cent female have low stress and low status. 18.9 per cent female have medium stress and medium status. 10.0 per cent female respondents have high stress and high status whereas 8.9 per cent female have high stress and medium status. The observed value of χ^2 (2.335) was non-significant at 5.0 per cent and 4 d.f. Variety is the spice of life. The sense of betrayal can feel overwhelming. With the betrayal in loss, grief, pain, self doubts, anger and guilt.

Table 5.23. Psychological stress of female as per economic status

Economic status	Psychological stress		
	Low	Medium	High
Low	9 (10.0)	12 (13.3)	17 (18.9)
Medium	6 (6.7)	17 (18.9)	8 (8.9)
High	6 (6.7)	6 (6.7)	9 (10.0)
χ^2	2.335	P > 0.05	

Figures in parentheses indicate percentage of respective values.

In Indian culture, man has to face a lot of difficulties in maintaining extra-marital relations in life. Because, in small society or community, the extra-marital relations can not be

hide for long period of time. At the time when these relations are exposed, the pressure from family as well as from society starts increasing. Children also do not feel convenient in accepting their parents with other partner. Due to which pressure from their children also interrupt them in maintaining their relations. For long period of time, unmarried partner can not go without marriage and after marriage these relations are discontinued.

CONSTRAINTS OF EXTRA-MARITAL RELATIONS TO MAINTAIN IN FUTURE RELATIONSHIP

Table 5.24 reveals that constraints of extra-marital relations to maintain in future maximum 70.7 per cent male respondents feels economic instability to maintain extra-marital relations in life followed by 50.7 per cent feels constraint like familiar pressure. 46.0 per cent male have faced social pressure in extra-marital relations to maintain in life. Minimum 37.3 per cent male respondents have faced tension of illegimate child to maintain relations. 75.5 per cent female respondents have faced maximum constraints due to family pressure in extra-marital relations to maintain

Table 5.24. Constraints of extra-marital relation to maintain in future relationship

Constrains	Male		Female	
	Fre-quency	Per cent	Fre-quency	Per cent
Social pressure	69	46.0	59	65.5
Family pressure	76	50.7	68	75.5
Economic instability	106	70.7	41	45.5
Tension of illegimate child	56	37.3	73	81.1
Stress due to marriage bond in women	—	—	64	71.1
Over demanding nature of partner	63	42.0	66	73.3

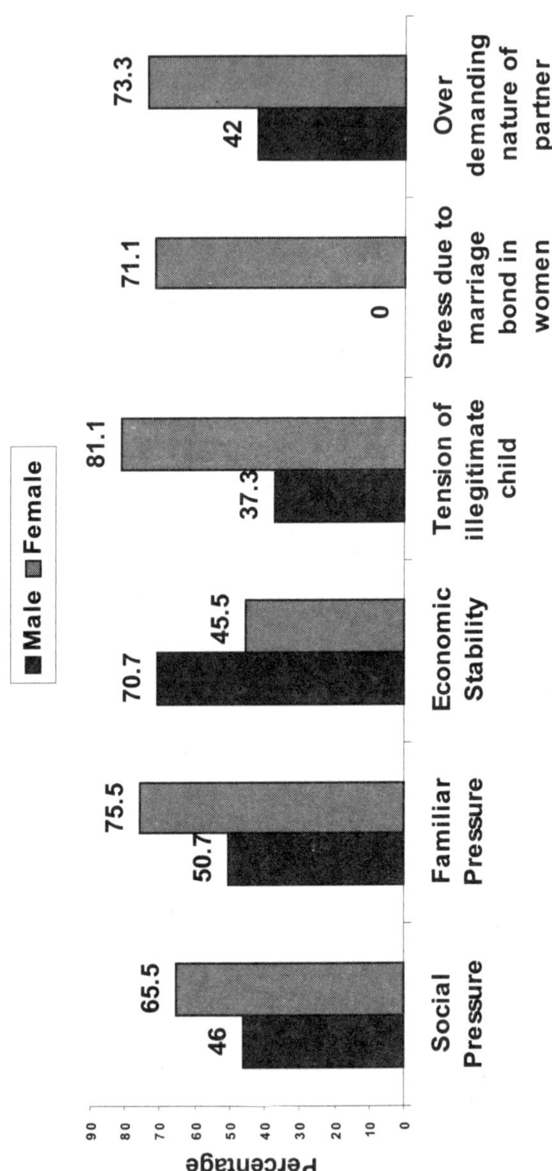

Fig. 5.14. Constraints of extra-marital to maintain in future relationship

in life. 73.3 per cent females have given the second highest percentage to over demanding nature of partner and this type of constraints more women faced who are engaged in extra-marital relations. 71.1 per cent women respondents have faced stress due to marriage bond in women in extra-marital relationship. 75.5 per cent women respondents have taking family pressure in family, children and society. 65.5 per cent women respondents have faced social pressure in society due to which she can not prolong extra-marital relationship in life.

Summary and Conclusion

Marriage is the unique bond between two people that links them together emotionally, spiritually and sexually in an enduring union based on common values, love and commitment. The circumstances that contribute to the fracturing of the intimate bond, *i.e.* an extra-marital relation, are diverse but most often involve transferring of emotional energy that was once directed to the marital harmony and for the family and children to other sources such as career and outside interests and friends. Under these conditions people may re-connect emotionally and spiritually with someone outside of their relationship by fulfilling ones need for acceptance and understanding. Extra marital relationships such as these begin benignly but may later evolve by becoming sexual posing a serious threat to the primary marital relationship.

Objectives

1. Socio-economic status of male and female.
2. Opinions of gender discrimination about extra-marital relations.
3. Assess the advantage and disadvantage of extra-marital relations.

4. Psychological stress of extra-marital relationship.
5. Constraints of extra-marital relations to maintain in future.

Research Methodology

The study was conducted in Kanpur district. Four zones were selected in the study area. 240 respondents (male and female both) were selected. Dependent and independent variables were used such as age, caste, education, sex, community opinion etc. The statistical tools as used such chi-square, weighted mean, percentage, correlation coefficient.

Major Findings

1. Maximum 38.7 per cent male belonged to 40 to 50 years age group whereas, 30.0 per cent male respondents belonged to 30 to 40 years age group, whereas, 41.1 per cent female respondents belong to 30 to 40 years age-group. 23.3 per cent female respondents belonged to 20 to 30 years age-group. Majority of the respondents (66.7%) belonged to middle age group (30 to 50 years). Age is an important factor in having extra-marital relationship. According to psychologists after 40 years, there is a psychological change occur in males that why extra-marital relation usually occur.
2. 37.3 per cent male respondents were educated up to graduate level whereas 24.0 per cent PG and above. 43.3 per cent female respondents were educated up to graduate level whereas 26.7 per cent female respondents have passed Intermediate. 39.6 per cent respondents have passed graduate and 20.0 per cent respondents have passed PG and above. Only education is not responsible for extra-marital relations. Because since ancient time in lower strata of society, lack of education extra-marital relation still persist in this strata.

3. 62.5 per cent male respondents and 37.5 per cent female respondents. Marital relationship are related to sex of the respondents are disharmony in married life, proximity at work place, high expectations from marriage, extended periods away form home, loneliness and depression, fulfilling a sexual fantasy, physical attraction, prolonged dating and sexual intimacy of people is common cause of developing extra-marital relationship. Extra-marital relationship were strongly influenced by the gender of the married individual.
4. 41.3 per cent male respondents belonged to upper caste whereas 32.0 per cent middle caste. 38.9 per cent female respondents belonged to upper caste whereas 32.2 per cent respondents were of lower category. Majority of 40.4 per cent respondents belonged to upper caste whereas 30.8 per cent belonged to middle category. Caste plays an important role in extra-marital relations of the respondents.
5. 52 per cent male respondents belonged Hindu religion whereas 22.7 per cent male respondents belonged Muslim religion. 52.2 per cent female respondents belonged to Hindu religion whereas 23.3 per cent female belonged Christian. More than fifty five per cent respondents belonged Hindu family while 17.9 per cent belonged to Muslim family. Minimum 12.5 per cent respondents belonged to Sikh religion.
6. 29.3 per cent male respondents have earned Rs. 30,000 and above, whereas 32.7 per cent male respondents have earned Rs. 10,000 to Rs. 20,000 monthly. 37.8 per cent female respondents have earned Rs. 20,000 to Rs. 30,000 monthly while 25.6 per cent female respondents have earned Rs. 30,000 and above monthly. 27.9 per cent respondents have earned Rs. 30,000 and above monthly followed

28.3 per cent respondents have earned Rs. 20,000 to Rs. 30,000 monthly. Minimum 14.6 per cent respondents have earned up to Rs. 10,000 monthly.

7. 18 per cent male belonged to high economic status whereas 46.0 per cent have medium economic status. 23.4 per cent female respondents belonged to high economic status while 34.4 per cent female have medium economic status. Minimum 42.2 per cent female respondents were from low economic status family. Overall 20 per cent respondents have high, 41.7 per cent medium and 38.3 per cent have low economic status.
8. Maximum more than forty per cent male respondents have participated and member of 3 to 4 organizations whereas, 29.3 per cent male respondents have member of 1 to 2 organizations. 46.7 per cent female respondents have a member of 3 to 4 organizations, whereas, 34.4 per cent female respondents have joined 1 to 2 organizations. Minimum 22.9 per cent respondents have joined 5 and more organization. Every human living in structured social groups, human have adhered to the belief that formal unions of two people work best for maintaining a healthy functioning society. Human being have been engaging in non-monogamous activities throughout history.
9. 62 per cent male and 36.7 per cent female have desired sexual addiction affair, sexual addicts use sex over and over again to numb inner pair and emptiness much like alcoholics use alcohol. Among married people, men are sexual addicts more often than women. 59.3 per cent male and 57.8 per cent female were showed intimacy avoidance affair are frightened of getting too close, so they keep the barriers high between them. 46 per cent male and 45.5 per cent female were showed conflict avoidance

affairs where they can't resolve their difference and the marriage erodes. 27.3 per cent male and 53.3 per cent female have split self affair tried to do marriage right. Only 42 per cent male and 41.1 per cent female were engaged in exit affair where in one spouse has already decided to leave the marriage and the affair provides the justification.

10. 24 per cent male respondents engaged more than one month towards attraction and 14.7 per cent male were engaged more than one year duration in friendship towards female. 28.7 per cent male have engaged up to 30 days in sexual relationship and 12 per cent male were involved more than one year in sexual relationship. 3.3 per cent female respondents were engaged in up to 30 days in attraction towards males whereas 23.3 per cent female were attracted for more than one month. 20.0 per cent female have attract towards male in friendship more than one month. 3.3 per cent female have taking sexual relationship up to one month whereas 17.8 per cent female have engaged in sexual relationship to male more than one month.

11. 74 per cent male and 74.4 per cent female have taking relationship as a fashion/status symbol whereas 70.7 per cent male and 52.2 per cent female were suffered disharmony in married life. 62.7 per cent male and 45.5 per cent female respondents were attracted towards opposite sex while 58 per cent male and 35.5 per cent female were unsatisfied from sexual relations, sex is perhaps one of the most important reasons why troubles start in relationships. 32 per cent male and 32.2 per cent female have suffered lack of love in married life, love like other emotions changes with time. 17.3 per cent male and 58.9 per cent female were suffering job tension whereas 51.1 per cent female and 14 per cent male have economic problem, remove these type of stress they link with

other opposite sex relationships to satisfy their sexual needs and orgasms such romance and sex addicts are usually driven by the passion they find in new relationships.

12. 50.7 per cent male and 72.2 female have given causes as dispute marriage itself is damaged or the relations between the two people are neglected and strained then it can result in people having affairs. 42 per cent male and 56.7 per cent female have reasons self-esteem problem and such individuals are not able to handle the usual problems in the relationship. 54.7 per cent male and 62.2 per cent female have desire for happiness, as the society progresses selfishness and an individualistic pattern of thinking has become the norm. 50.7 per cent male and 15.6 per cent female have disappointment that one partner hasn't grown in the same way, women seen to be drawn into adulterous relationships initially through emotional attachments while men are more likely attracted sexually. 16.0 per cent male and 44.4 per cent female have inability to cope with cultural or ethnic differences in their sex drive and in the sex drive of their partner, one partner withhold sex or shows little interest the other partner may fill that need outside the marriage.
13. 76.7 per cent women have attracted towards many in extra-marital affair because the other person is rich and they can enjoy many things in life which they otherwise cannot afford. 81.1 per cent female respondents have feel problems in relationship, this may be frequent arguments with current life partner or could be stress over children. 62.2 per cent female like married men because women are emotional and they often feel married men can understand their feelings much better in comparison to the bachelors. 21.1 per cent women may engage in a relationship for promotion or for a raise in her life. 34.4 per cent

women find having sex with new partners as exciting and may fulfill their hidden fantasies.

14. 91.3 per cent men respondents were attract towards beauty of women, whereas 88 per cent male attract towards sex appeal of women. 81.3 per cent men always like unmarried young girl, because they attracted and wishes to have unwanted relationship. 62.0 per cent men attracted towards physical attraction of women, the men who get into a love marriage often laments that, they had only seen the good side of their partner prior to marriage. 46.7 per cent men wanted extra-marital affairs due to power and job status while 43.3 per cent men wanted other relations due to illness of his wife in sex or other diseases in body the situations becomes worse as they do not receive due support from their partners, they may find an outsource to cry out their dilemmas, who may better understood the true feelings thus person engaged in sexual activity with someone other than their marriage partner.

15. 86 per cent male and 76.7 per cent female have suffered disharmony in married life whereas 72 per cent male and 45.5 per cent female were invite extra-marital relationship for fulfilling a sexual fantasy. 54.7 per cent male and 42.2 per cent female have attracted towards physical looking whereas 47.3 per cent male and only 13.3 per cent female were used relationship for revival of an old flame. 48 per cent male and 65.5 per cent female were engaged extra-marital relationship who lived long periods away from home.

16. 52.7 per cent male were given opinion maintain personality whereas 46.7 per cent female respondents maintain personality in extra-marital relationship. 42.7 per cent male and 32.2 per cent female respondents increase their work efficiency due to

extra-marital relations. 73.3 per cent male respondents have believed in living and 70 per cent female have believed in living whatever they wants they do. 50.7 per cent male and 37.8 per cent female have reduced stress when they engaged opposite sex friendship and extra-marital relationship. In opposite sex relations they feel happy. 28.7 per cent male and 47.8 per cent female have feel more caring in extra-marital relations. 59.3 per cent male and 60.0 per cent female were reduced loneliness with the help of extra-marital relations.

17. 50.0 per cent female have feeling insecure due to environment and society culture. 66 per cent male respondents have feel sexual transmitted diseases like HIV/AIDS whereas 47.8 per cent female respondents feared catching a sexually transmitted disease. Over 67.4 per cent male said that they had changed their behaviours because of the AIDS scare. 80.7 per cent male respondents have given ripple effect in life whereas 62.2 per cent female respondents have given ripple effect in life, extra-marital affairs can cause a ripple effect in life, this can be either positive or negative, but most respondents of an affair say that it brought on changes in all other areas of their lives. 30.7 per cent male have fear about extra-marital relationship whereas 41.1 per cent female have fear about relationship hence less relationship.

18. 46.0 per cent male were affected by damage of self-esteem whereas 61.1 per cent female respondents were effected due to self-esteem. 68 per cent male have lack of trust in extra-marital relation whereas 57.8 per cent female have faced lack of trust. 38 per cent male respondents have faced sense of instability whereas 73.3 per cent female have face sense of instability. 62 per cent male respondents have roller-coaster of emotion whereas 91.1 per cent female respondents have suffering in emotions in extra-

marital relationships. 48 per cent male respondents have affected loss of passion due to psychological stress. Female have less loss of passion in comparison to male. Female have 87.8 per cent mental insecure, which is too high in comparison to male, 65.3 per cent male feel economic insecure due to expenditure of extra-marital relation. 70 per cent female and 74 per cent male have feel social pressure due to fear in extra-marital relationship.

19. 40.7 per cent male and 74.4 per cent female were suffering mental stress whereas 32 per cent male and 80.0 per cent female have faced loneliness. 61.3 per cent male and 43.3 per cent female have used extra marital relationship due to economic status, whereas 52.7 per cent male and 46.7 per cent female were having dating in extra-marital relationship exhibit his or her personality. 61.7 per cent children have feels loneliness due to their parent's nature while 54.6 per cent children have faced mental stress due to loneliness and discarded by parents. 50.8 per cent whole family gone in mental stress.

20. 48.0 per cent male and 81.1 per cent female have suffered depression in extra-marital relationship. 46.0 per cent male and 47.8 per cent female respondents were feeling guilty in extra-marital relationship. 11.3 per cent male and 56.7 per cent respondents have felt mentally insecure in extra-marital relationship. 57.3 per cent male and 58.9 per cent female respondents have taking stress towards loneliness in extra-marital relationship.

21. 62 per cent male were commitment for open relations whereas 74.4 per cent female were given same stress. 65.3 per cent male were given more than one relationship, generally male have wants to more relations in opposite sex to remove his stress. Male does not want any expectation to his partner besides

sexual relations so this is one cause to remove his stress. 92.2 per cent ladies have engaged in work herself to remove psychological stress and 84.4 per cent ladies do not have any expectations to her partner in sexual relations. 74.4 per cent female commit for open relations to remove her psychological stress.

22. Four per cent male have low stress and high status while 10.7 per cent male have low stress and medium status. 20.7 per cent male have medium stress and medium status. 10.7 per cent male respondents have high stress and high status whereas 14.7 per cent male have high stress and medium status. 17.3 per cent male have high stress and low status.
23. 6.7 per cent female have low stress and high status while 10 per cent female have low stress and low status. 18.9 per cent female have medium stress and medium status. 10 per cent female respondents have high stress and high status whereas 8.9 per cent female have high stress and medium status.
24. Maximum 70.7 per cent male respondents feels economic instability to maintain extra-marital relations in life followed by 50.7 per cent feels constraint like familiar pressure. 46 per cent male have faced social pressure in extra-marital relations to maintain in life. Minimum 37.3 per cent male respondents have faced tension of illegimate child to maintain relations. 75.5 per cent female respondents have faced maximum constraints due to family pressure in extra-marital relations to maintain in life. 73.3 per cent females have given the second highest percentage to over demanding nature of partner and this type of constraints more women faced who are engaged in extra-marital relations. 71.1 per cent women respondents have faced stress due to marriage bond in women in extra-marital relation-

ship. 75.5 per cent women respondents have taking family pressure in family, children and society. 65.5 per cent women respondents have faced social pressure in society due to which she can not prolong extra-marital relationship in life.

Suggestions, Recommendation and Policy Implications

1. The more positive a woman's attitude toward sex, the longer she continued the extra-marital relationship.
2. Office romances are generally believed to be unhelpful to the welfare and effectiveness of the business and to the network of relationship that comprise it.
3. Office romance is bound to happen. If you have people sharing common interest (work) + extended time together (40 h) + physical attraction = a perfect match.
4. Nothing wrong with office romance and it is actually a good thing, because some one looks forward to going to work to see higher crush. He/she think that the consulting industry has the highest rate of office romance because one is constantly out on the road, and it can get pretty lonely.
5. Usually office behaviour/personality carries over to the private life. If someone is courteous, understanding, outgoing, etc. they will be that way in a romantic relationship as well and one can typically spend 8-12 hours at work and it is a very good way to get to know someone.
6. A part from all the consequences extra-marital relations is one of the major factor, which strengthen the relation between husband and wife, because they have a fear of cheating and insecurity.

7. Any of the spouses who are likely to be more romantic, it is considered that he/she has lesser chances of disease because he/she always stays happy.
8. It is seen that before extra-marital relations, married life is a little boring because spouse is less concern, but after developing extra-marital relations he/she also moves towards more of family responsibility. Thus, it's better to work harder.
9. It also said that the person who is having extra-marital relations is less likely to have heart disease.

Bibliography

Adrian, J. Blow and MC Gannon Hall (2005). Infidelity in committed relationships II : A substantive Review. *Journal of Marital and Family Therapy,* **31**(2) : 217-233, doi : 10.

Anon, Paris and Anon (2000). A expriences of falling in love. *Journal of Social and Personal Relationship* **6**, 243-257. Journals /Org/ production/action/ Fulltext.

Atkins and Dimidijan (2001). The dynamics, implications and treatment of extra-marital sexual relatioonships for the family therapist". *Journal of Marital and Family Therapy,* **7**(4) : 489-495 doi : 10.

Bhattacharjee, J. and Gupta, R.S. (2000). *Pre and extra-marital heterosexual behaviour.*

Bienko, M. (1999). *International Journal of Law, Policy and the Family.*

Broode, J. (2000). Article on extra-marital affair.

Buss and Schmitt (2004). Sexual strategies theory, *Psychological Review, 100,* 209-232.

Durex's (2001). *The Global Sex Survey.*

Fehr (1999). An interpersonal theory analysis.

Fred, P. Piercy (2003). *Internet Infidelity : A Critical review of literature.*

Glass and Wright (1999). Justificaitons for extra-marital relaitonships: The associaiton between attitudes, behaviour and gender. *Journal of Sex Research.*

Greg, Swenson (2005). Coping with infidelity in marriage.

Joyneer and Udry (2000). Consequences in Extra-marital affair. Extra-marital relation and depression. *Journal of Health and Social Bheaviour,* **41.**

Kienlen (2006). Reasons for extra-marital affairs.

Kinsey *et al.* (2002). Extra-marital sex : Prevalence and correlates in a national survey.

Kirn, Clay (2000). *Monitor on psychology* 20-33.

Layton, Debbie (2002). Extra-marital Affair.

Mayering, Ralph A. (2001). *The future of marriage.*

Megan, Sweeny (2003). Extra-marital sex.

Menagham, Elizabeth G. (2008). Depressive affect and subsequent divorce.

Meyer, Cathy (1999). *Impact of extra-marital affairs.*

Misha, Safranski (2009). How does an extra-marital affair affect families?

Mortimer and Sorenson (1999). Women's Employment and Family Relations : *Journal of Marriage and Family.*

Pawlik, Laurie (2007). *Emotional cheating.*

Powell, Bline (2007). *What causes affair.*

Priya Devi R. (2006). *Extra-marital affairs at their excellence.*

Regan (2000). Document on love and affair.

Roid, Anna (2009). Should marital infidelity necessarily lead to divorce?

S.P. and Wright (2002). Extra-marital affair.

Sanjeev Sharma (2005). Extra-marital-affair.

Sharma, Sanjeev (1999). Article of extra-marital affairs.

Shirley and Thomas (1999). Traditional sex Roles : *Journal on Sex Roles.*

Singh, Bir, (2002). Sex and marriage Counselling clinic. All India Institute of Medical Sciences, New Delhi.

Smith, Lovin, Lynn (2007). "The sociology of affect and emotion".

Smith, Robert E. (2008). Concordia theological seminar.

Soulen (2008). "Marriage and Divorce – Problem in New Testament Interpretation".

Sprecher, Susan (2000). Sex roles : A Journal of Research.

Strean, Herbert (2003). Psychoanalytic Review LXIII, 2003. *The Extra-marital Relation.*

Vaughan, Peggy (2002). Article on extra-marital affairs.

Victor, A. *Petrak and Don Mortin* (2004).

Walster, Elaine and G. William Walster (2002). Article equity and extra-marital sexuality.

Weis and Jurich (2000).

Wiederman, Michael W. (2001). The *journal of marriage and family*.

Wiederman, Michael W. (2001). The Journal of sex research.

Wiser, Bud (2007). *The-Anatomy of an Affair-review.*

Wittkower, E.D. (1999). *Effect of extra-marital affair happen* ?

Zinskin and Zinskin (2000). Emotinal and sexual component of Extra-marital relation.

Index